GRANTED

A PRO SE GUIDE TO OBTAINING PAROLE

BY: RAYMOND E. LUMSDEN

"Education and action makes a people easy to lead, but difficult to drive; easy to govern, but impossible to enslave and incarcerate."
- Lord Henry Brougham

Freebird Publishers
www.FreebirdPublishers.com

Freebird Publishers
221 Pearl St. Ste. 541, North Dighton, MA 02764
Info@FreebirdPublishers.com
www.FreebirdPublishers.com

Granted: A Pro Se Guide To Obtaining Parole
By Raymond E. Lumsden

All Freebird Publishers titles, imprints, and distributed lines are available at special quantity discounts for bulk purchases for sales promotions, premiums, fundraising, educational, or institutional use.

ISBN: 978-1-952159-53-4

Printed in the United States of America

DEDICATION ★★★

It would be impossible for me to list everyone who should be included in this dedication. There simply wouldn't be enough paper. So, I'll focus on the most deserving.

First and foremost, as always, to my children, Anthony, Alyssa, Joshua, and Rylee, who are now adults and teens. Without you, nothing about me makes sense, and I serve no other purpose. Distance separates us, but love and family always keep us right where we belong: Together.

To Melissa Williams, who has stood beside me and supported me in ways I could never explain. You are a blessing.

To the educators at the Colleges and Universities who taught me the law, how to fight, when to fight, and everything that I know and pass along to you in my writings.

To my Mother, Roxanne, the first and greatest love of my life. Hands down, the strongest person I have ever known and the person responsible for every achievement I have ever known. I love you, Mom.

And finally, to all of the incarcerated seeking to obtain relief and parole by educating themselves properly. I say this, and mean this: NEVER EVER EVER GIVE UP!! Life only brings you what you are willing to accept, so refuse to accept anything less than what you want and deserve.

Education. Dedication. Expectation.

LEGAL NOTICE: This book is written and/or published by prisoners and concerned American Citizens. The law prohibits us from providing any legal advice to prisoners. This information is not intended as legal advice or representation, nor should you consider or rely upon it as such. Neither the organization of these people nor any information contained herein is intended to or shall constitute a contract between us and the readers; furthermore, we do not guarantee the accuracy of the court recordings contained in any court. Additionally, your use of this publication should not be construed as creating any relationship with anyone involved with us or anyone whose name may or may not appear in these court filings. Finally, while all provided information was up to date at the time of publication, we cannot guarantee that all information is still current at the time you read this.

★★★ TABLE OF CONTENTS ★★★

Dedication iii
Introduction 1
Chapter 1 Preparing The Parole Packet 3
Chapter 2 Prison Life: Punishment vs. Opportunity 7
Chapter 3 Planning & Organizing 11
Chapter 4 Texas Parole: The Unicorn 27
Chapter 5 Parole Appeal 175
Glossary of Terms 196
A Moment with the Author 202
About the Author 207

INTRODUCTION ★★★

This book is written for a simple purpose: to help you obtain parole and release, to restore your freedom even in the face of indigence that prevents you from hiring a parole lawyer.

Before I begin, let me first say this:

IF YOU CAN AFFORD A PAROLE ATTORNEY, HIRE ONE!!!

While I am attempting to walk you through the steps necessary to prepare and advance a successful parole packet, I do not intend to circumvent the hiring of a Licensed and Experienced Attorney in the event that you can afford to hire one. However, with my decade of experience in the prison system, most inmates simply cannot afford an attorney, so let's get started.

Throughout this book, I intend to provide you with the specific and exact information you need to obtain parole. These documents and records are mostly free, easy to prepare, and readily accessible, which will allow you and your friends or family to design and prepare a parole packet that will work.

Well, give you a higher percentage to work, anyway. As you know, there are no guarantees in prison.

My sole intent here is to give you a generalized overview of current laws, statutes, and eligibility requirements related to parole. Of course, these are different in every state, and you must conduct some research. However, the parole packet, as I designed for you here, will work the same in every state.

The book contains a plethora of information for my Texas fellow inmates. Since I am here in Texas, it is also available to you in other states if you write a letter requesting it from the Parole Board, etc. For me to have obtained it from every state for the purpose of this book would have taken hundreds of thousands of pages, an act of futility in the writing of it. Yes, you are going to have to do a little research and work if you are not in Texas, but that’s okay: No pain, no gain.

Keep in mind that all state parole boards are more than a year behind in releasing updated parole numbers, statistics, and information. What I have included here, are the most recent and correct available.

Parole

CHAPTER 1

PREPARING THE PAROLE PACKET

The sole purpose of preparing a parole packet is to present it on your behalf to the parole board, which is tasked with considering your release to parole. In states like Minnesota, my home state, parole packets are unnecessary since your release date is determined the minute you enter the prison system. There are no questions about when you will be released; thus, you do no need to worry about a parole board since there isn't one.

However, in states like Texas, where parole is like a Unicorn, often heard of but rarely seen, if ever, a parole packet is not only necessary but vital. It is your chance to demonstrate to the parole board of highly conservative and judgmental individuals who would rather keep you in prison that you have learned from the act that brought you to prison and that you have made good use of your prison time, etc.

The sole purpose is to promote yourself to the parole board, which you will rarely see in person, through the information and documentation within the parole packet. What's more, and far more importantly, it is to convince the parole board that you are committed to staying out of prison if released and enough so that you took the time to put the parole packet together in the first place.

Trust me, it matters.

Now, let me show you what is inside of the parole packet.

A. Your statement (inmate)

   1. Background

Here, you should provide the personal information necessary to confirm your identity: name, identification number, date and place of birth, parents' information, etc.

Next, you get a bit more personal and provide information that you have likely learned to keep private and protected while incarcerated: where you were raised, who you lived with growing up, the names of your siblings, where you went to school, the degrees and certifications you have earned, previous jobs or military experience, etc.

You should also come clean since they likely already know more about you than you know about yourself, and tell them about prior arrests, convictions, and prison stays.

Tell the parole board about your lifestyle and the circumstances of the prior bad acts, convictions, and prison sentences in your past. Be sure to include a detailed summary of it all to show the parole board that you are aware of your bad behavior and that you own it.

DO NOT LEAVE ANYTHING OUT, or they will think you are hiding it from them in an attempt to manipulate the system. Honesty is a character of change and responsibility that is essential to obtaining parole in any state parole system.

Keep in mind, and I cannot express this enough: no matter how slick and deceptive you might believe and think that you are, the parole board will absolutely have all, and I mean ALL of your records to include from other states, SO BE OPEN AND HONEST.

Do not attempt to explain away or defend from the past history you might have. List everything you can remember and let them know that you may have forgotten and not intentionally left out information, etc.

Current Conviction:

You cannot avoid it, and you cannot hide from it. You MUST account for the behavior and crime that sent you to prison in the instant. And, you must OWN it.

Begin by describing the crime that caused your arrest and prison sentence. My advice is not to defend yourself but to list the offense exactly as it was detailed at your trial or in the State's Brief on appeal, word-for-word, since that is the only way the parole board will see it.

This is not what they expect, and honestly, that will go far in demonstrating that you not only own your behavior but have also learned from it. This is vital.

Parole consideration does not mean you are being found guilty again or facing additional punishment. The worst has already been done, and parole consideration is not only a blessing to you; it is a demonstration that you have represented and carried yourself in a manner worthy of parole, which is a tribute to your character.

By lying to the parole board or attempting to minimize your crime or actions that landed you in prison, the parole board will see you as attempting to manipulate them and that you lack any sense of remorse and accountability for your behavior.

Let me say it better this way: *OWN YOUR ACTIONS.*

Even if you feel that you are innocent (I will address that later in the book), that witnesses testified falsely against you, that the authorities got the wrong person or gave a false report, or whatever else you feel strongly about...**OWN IT**.

When describing your crime, do so exactly as it was detailed against you by the prosecution or at your trial. This will give you credibility with the parole board, trust me.

Detail the crime as it happened while taking full accountability and responsibility for having committed it. Show that you are remorseful for your actions and those that were perhaps hurt by your actions. Follow that up by telling and then showing the parole board what you have done while in prison to change your behavior that will keep you from offending again if released.

Talk about your victims if you have them. List their names to demonstrate that you know who they are and that you have been affected by and are remorseful for how you impacted their lives. I can tell you that most inmates cannot remember the names of their victims, and you will be well-received if you can.

For most crimes having been committed under the effects of drugs and/or alcohol, be sure to detail any and all of the classes and treatment courses/programs that you have taken while in prison. And, there *SHOULD* be if you are truly serious about ever making parole. Detail your attendance and participation in those programs, and more importantly, tell the parole board how they affected you and incorporated change in your life.

No matter what you say, it is of the utmost importance to always, always, always refrain from expressing anything that might be perceived by the parole board as denying accountability or responsibility for your actions, behavior, and the crime that landed you in prison.

One more time: *OWN YOUR SHIT.*

After further consideration, I have decided to go ahead and address the idea of "innocence" here, now, since most inmates, if not all, believe they are innocent and will tell the parole board that they are, *which is a grave mistake.*

I have never heard of nor researched any factual claims where a parole board granted parole to any inmate who stood on their innocence at the review. As stated, parole boards not only want but EXPECT you to admit your behavior and the crime that landed you in prison and, more importantly, to show that you have remorse for it.

If you are truly innocent, which I can relate to as detailed in the book *The Scales of Injustice: The Raymond Lumsden Story*, written by investigative Author Marian D. Wiljohn about my own wrongful arrest and conviction, here is my advice...

Begin by expressing remorse about the entire event, such as the police intervention and involvement, the prosecution burden that wasted taxpayer dollars, and even any perceived burdens felt by the compliant (never use the word victim if you are truly innocent).

Express your remorse for the events without taking any personal responsibility or account for the crime itself, and then stop right there. Do not assert your innocence repeatedly, or the results will not be in your favor; I can promise you that.

For instance, let's say that you are in prison for Capital Murder, which I know does not even provide for parole eligibility. You would say something like this:

> "I am terribly sorry for the loss of Mr. Johnson's life as well as the effect that it has likely had on his family. Such loss is always a tragedy, and I have tremendous empathy and sympathy for all parties involved."

That's that. Enough said.

CHAPTER 2

PRISON LIFE: PUNISHMENT VS. OPPORTUNITY

Make no mistake, most law enforcement authorities, as well as parole board members, believe that prison is intended for and meant as punishment for your crimes. They do not even give consideration to the fact that a convicted person might perceive it as an opportunity. More so, as having perhaps saved their life.

Thus, you must demonstrate to the parole board all of the benefits, opportunities, and character-building tools that incarceration presented to you, making you a better person now than you were when you entered prison.

Think about it, which you likely never have before: are you not a better person than you were when you entered prison?

By maturity alone, I'd argue and suggest that you are, but there are much more powerful examples that you can provide.

Tell and show the parole board all the hard work you have put in during your incarceration. All of the personal sacrifices and dedication you have put forth to change your thinking and behavior. To overcome addictions and to ascend your education and vocational understandings.

Prison is not easy, and there are many negative distractions that the parole board is certainly aware of. The prison environment in the "inmate code" context is set up for failure. However, the opportunities provided through education, vocation, treatment, sobriety, etc., are designed for your success if you choose or choose to utilize them. The parole board will easily and quickly determine which relates to you.

Overcoming boundaries and hurdles requires strength, perseverance, and dedication, and the parole board will want to see that in your packet. It is not only important, but it is also crucial that you show the parole board what you have done every day of your prison life and how it has affected not only you but also those around you inside and outside of prison.

a. Prison Accomplishments

Your parole packet must include your educational certificates and degrees earned during incarceration. Also important are any vocational (bricklaying, HVAC, Computer, Braille, etc.) Certificates and degrees you obtained during incarceration. Parole Boards tend to emphasize therapeutic programming and participation, such as AA, NA, SOTP, and any/all other therapeutic and treatment-type classes or live-in environments. For instance, here in Texas, there is a Drug Recovery Program in certain prisons that offers a drug-free, therapeutic live-in housing program for inmates who struggle with and from addictions.

Jarrod Brown, an inmate Peer Coach at the Hughes Unit, facilitates the peer-driven curriculum. He is Certified and Licensed to teach by the Texas Department of Criminal Justice.

Jarrod is a former drug addict and understands the hardship, struggle, and consequences that addictions have on human lives. In fact, it was drug addiction that caused Jarrod to be arrested and sentenced to prison for drug-related crimes. He, an honorably discharged Veteran from a good family with all of the opportunity in the world, was unable to overcome the addiction that nearly ruined his life permanently.

When he came to prison, he did what all inmates should do: Realize that something has to be changed, seek out and inquire about programs and classes available to bring forth that change, and immediately register to take them all.

Jarrod, along with a handful of other Peer Coaches in the TDCJ system, turned the script on the drug addictions that once controlled and dominated their lives and now teaches that recovery process to other inmates who are exactly where they once were.

He is not only a Peer Coach (Recovery) but also licensed and certified by the State. This means that upon his release from prison in the coming months, he will be able to have a new career previously unavailable to him that will help save lives. In fact, as Jarrod currently prepares his own parole packet for review, he can include a formal letter of employment by the United States Veteran's Administration (VA) to teach and assist drug-addicted veterans outside of prison.

He did exactly what you can do: Take your weakness and make it your strength to help others. And then show it to the parole board.

- Prison Jobs: List all of the jobs you have had during your incarceration, and be sure to emphasize those you have held for a long time.
- Volunteer: List all of the volunteer activities you have participated in, such as P.A.C.E., JAYCEES, etc.

If you have it, make specific intent to relate and also demonstrate any leadership roles that you have held and maintained while in prison. Tell the parole board what your leadership role(s) encompassed, including service roles to the inmate population, administration, etc.

And, of course, with the goodwill, sometimes comes the bad. After the good, be sure to address the bad, AKA your prison disciplinary history. If it is lengthy and extensive, which will not help you much in parole consideration, try to demonstrate, if possible, how maybe most of them occurred at the beginning of the prison term and improved or ended as you adjusted and began to focus on change.

Show the parole board your behavioral improvements, even if they are small in nature. Maybe you used to get into a lot of fights when you first arrived in prison, but then that ended, and you had a struggle with drug use. Then, demonstrate how you overcame the drug use but then found yourself violating a rule for being where you aren't supposed to be (out of place), etc.

Better yet, and more hopeful for you, if you have no disciplinary history during your prison term, emphasize how that reflects your willingness to follow the rules and your ability to conform to and follow parole requirements if granted.

Remember that parole board members are not stupid and have lengthy experience dealing with inmates of all types. There is nothing that you can say or do that will surprise them or mislead them. So, keep it honest, real, and direct.

b. Parole Plan

This may be the most important part of the parole packet, next to your prison conduct and accomplishments. If you are granted parole, it tells the parole board the detailed plans for your release back into society.

Letters from potential employers, family members with whom you can live or who will offer support, friends, religious clergy or ministers, mental health professionals, etc. Is anyone ready and willing to provide you with support?

If you have plans to participate in counseling programs when you are released, for instance, any AA or NA treatment classes or programs (which you should have already located, contacted, and received letters from), you should tell the parole board about them. Again, if you did not hear my hint, be sure to make contact with these treatment facilities and programs *BEFORE* your parole review arrives so that you can obtain recommendation letters and participation acceptance and assure the parole board that there is room and availability for your participation.

This demonstrates priority and planning, both of which they will reward you for in the decision process.

c. Parole Packet Attachments

Initially and up to this point, you have been presenting to the parole board information and descriptions of yourself, a crime that sent you to prison, prison accomplishments, and achievements, and your plans for release should you be granted parole.

The documents supporting and proving your statements are the attachments you will include with the parole packet statements. They are essentially the "put up or shut up" part of the parole packet.

While not exhaustive, the following is a list of documents that should be included as attachments and labeled clearly for the parole board to review. If there are more than I have listed below and you wish for the parole board to consider them, then add them:

- *Resume:* See the sample I have included in the Appendix
- *Educational:* Copies of your GED or other prison-earned degrees or certificates.
- *Vocational:* Copies of all vocational-related certificates earned while in prison.
- *Therapeutic*: Copies of all certificates of the programs you've taken and completed while in prison.
- *Volunteer:* Copies of any/all certificates of participation or commendation you received during your prison term.
- *Support Letters:* See my example in the Appendix.

Now, we will roll up our sleeves and get into the meat and potatoes of a strong parole packet….so let's get started.

CHAPTER 3
PLANNING & ORGANIZING

In order to write an effective and winning parole packet, you must plan and organize it first. As I pointed out previously, the parole board will already have before it the following:

- Criminal history report;
- Prosecutor's comments;
- Trial-related documents;
- Victim impact statements and stance towards your release to parole;
- Police Report, Indictment;
- Your prison record and disciplinary report;
- Etc.

It is important and imperative that your parole packet be in the hands of the parole board no less than six (6) months before your parole review. Keep in mind that the parole board can and will probably hold a review of your parole earlier than you are expecting. Without your parole packet to consider, they are more than likely to deny rather than grant parole, especially here in Texas.

You need the parole packet to offer adversarial evidence to the negative evidence and information about you that they already possess and will use to determine whether to grant you parole or not. Without it, the parole board will have only negative information about you.

The parole packet is vital to making you seem more "human" in the eyes of the parole board, which is usually biased towards inmates. This is represented by the extremely low number of parole granted across the country, specifically here in Texas.

A well-planned and organized parole package will be compiled in the following manner: Introduction letter;

- Cover (Picture of you included);
- Table of contents;
- Educational & Vocational Certifications;
- Parole Plan;
- Resume;
- Support letters;
- Employment or Treatment Letters;
- Photos.

The purpose of the photos included on the Cover Page is that the parole board will only have your prison photo available for review. As we all know, prison photos are biased since most prisons require that you not smile, and any reflection of your disposition is hidden.

Photos of you in the context of freedom, wearing the same clothes as them, eating at the same restaurants as them, and doing the same events, hobbies, and fun-related things as they help the parole board see you for what/who you are: *a human being*.

Let's take it step-by-step now and put it all together.

a. What to Include in the Letter of Support

First, the person writing the letter should detail the nature of their relationship with you, such as Son, Daughter, Husband, Wife, Brother, Sister, Cousin, Neighbor, Friend, Pastor, Etc.

Then, they should include information for the parole board, such as how long they have known you, some good qualities that they personally know you have, their familiarity with your crime, and any demonstrated remorse you've shown them.

More importantly, they should write about their personal knowledge of your prison-related positivity. Things you have done during your incarceration, programs you have participated in successfully, addiction-related classes and programs, any and all classes related to alternatives to violence, etc.

They should make every effort to portray you as a human being, that you are more than just the worst moment in your life, and that your past behavior and actions do not define who you are or what you are capable of accomplishing.

The person writing the letter of support for you should take it one step further, if willing, and provide detailed information related to them personally. Information shows that they are respected in the community, business, or church. This will lend credibility to them and a strong basis for them to provide you with the support necessary for a successful transition into the community on parole.

Sometimes, which is quite often the case with inmates, good people commit dumb crimes. The person writing the letter of support for you can tell the parole board about your long-standing in the community for good prior to your prison sentence. This is powerful information for the parole board.

No matter what the person writes in their support letter, it should never include anything that might be perceived as minimizing the seriousness of the crime or promoting and citing your innocence. Even if they truly believe that you are, in fact, innocent, their letter is not the right place to address it.

They should also not attack police, investigators, or the courts since some parole board members are previous members of those occupations. To do so would ensure your denial of parole.

b. The Parole Interview

Like it or not, ready or not, you will have to be interviewed by a parole officer while on the prison grounds. This serves two important and primary purposes: (1) to convince the parole board that you are ready to be released into society; (2), should you be denied parole, provide a record for any appeal you might want to make.

Unless you are a professional speaker and used to stressful presentations, you are expected to be nervous during your parole interview. Who wouldn't be, right?

But this is critical, and you should rehearse that interview with a trusted peer, teacher, minister, or even with a family member or friend during a visit. Your parole interview is your one chance to be heard before the decision is handed down.

Be well prepared and, more importantly, rehearsed.

The parole interview will begin with the parole officer asking you many questions after they have made a proper introduction. If allowed, shake their hand while maintaining eye contact as a show of respect.

Shaking hands while looking into the eyes of the person with whose hand you are shaking sets the tone for establishing you as a human being, an individual, and a well-mannered one.

Shake their hand firmly but not aggressively, and always refer to them as Ma'am or Sir.

Do not sit down until after they have done so, as this will be perceived as a sign of respect for authority.

Before heading to the parole hearing, let me tell you the most frequently used statements that a parole board uses to justify the denial of parole to an inmate: (1) It's unlikely that you will abide by the law upon release due to past criminal history; (2) You are a threat to society, and (3) Due to the seriousness of the crime.

Knowing this, you should be prepared to counter those expected findings long before the interview. Be prepared by speaking their language and using the statutory terms. For instance, referring to "your institutional record to include program goals (ITP) and accomplishments, academic achievements, vocational education, and work assignments."

Do not be an overachiever and talk yourself into a bad place; let the parole officer ask the questions, and you answer. While you must answer the questions, it is not necessary for you to provide information that you were never asked.

Speak of your release plans, community resources, employment, education, training or vocational, and support you will receive.

When asked questions, have a copy of your parole packet with you and refer to documents inside, such as certificates, participation letters, programming, etc. When asked hard questions about your crime or prison history, refer to programming you have taken successfully and the change you received from it.

Yes, you have a heavy burden in convincing the parole board to grant parole. But your parole packet contains all the information and documentation supporting that conviction.

Let's get you prepared for those hard questions, shall we?

i. FREQUENTLY ASKED QUESTIONS IN PAROLE REVIEW

- Why did you go to trial?
- Why did you take a plea of guilt?
- Why were you robbing people or hurting people?
- Why were you using drugs?
- How do you explain your violent history?
- How can we be assured that you will not return to your criminal activity if granted parole?
- What classes have you taken in prison that have made the biggest impression?
- Are you a gang member?
- Why do you feel you should be granted parole?
- Why should we take a chance on you?
- Are you lying to me now?
- Is there anything that you would like to add?

That last question. "Is there anything you would like to add?" is always the last question you will be asked. No matter what you are feeling, *You should always answer it with more information.* Again, this is your only chance to argue for your parole.

Summarize what you have already said, and refer to your parole packet documents and information once more, turning the pages as you do. Be sure to ask the parole officer, "After you have reviewed my case and spoken to me today, are there any concerns you have that might affect your decision related to my parole opportunity?"

This will provide you with a documented response on the record and allow you to appeal a denial. It is very important.

Now, let's get into a few of the Do's and Don'ts of the parole hearing…

ii. Do's

- Take charge of the hearing by being prepared;
- Be clear, concise, and direct;
- Accept responsibility;
- Never bring up negative things; let the parole officer bring them up first;
- If you do not understand the question, ask them to rephrase it so you can understand it;
- Correct any and all mistakes or misinformation related to your history or prison record.

iii. Don'ts

- "I'm sorry" isn't good enough. Express your remorse in a stronger manner;
- Don't follow the parole officer's script; make them follow yours by taking charge of the hearing in a positive manner;
- Never say that you "made a mistake." You committed a crime in their eyes, not a mistake. They expect you to own it.
- Do not follow the "Shawshank" example and tell the parole officer that you do not care if your parole is granted or not;
- Never feel intimidated or afraid to voice your feelings or correct misinformation.

In following the planning and organizing of the parole packet, there is a list of documents and records that you should have prior to attending your parole interview/hearing. These will not be included in your parole packet but are necessary to correct misinformation that the parole board might take into consideration:

- Pre-Sentence Report (PSR): Your trial court or attorney will have this; a letter should be written to obtain it.
- Sentencing Sheet: To prove your sentence.
- Prior Parole Records: Can be obtained through the parole department via letter.
- Criminal History: Can be obtained by the Court or your trial lawyer.

It is critical that you request and obtain these records well before you are scheduled for parole review to ensure enough time to receive and evaluate them, at least six (6) months before your parole hearing.

All in all, you have a better chance of being granted parole if you are prepared and prepared early. You should be able to recite your parole packet from memory if possible; that's how well you should know the material inside of it and hold “rehearsal” parole hearings/interviews with people you trust.

Now, let me show you what a Sample Parole Packet should look like and what should be included…

Notes:

[SAMPLE COVER LETTER]

02, October, 2023

Texas Department of Criminal Justice
c/o Pardons and Parole
P.O. Box 13401
Capitol Station
Austin, Texas, 78711-3401

RE: Parole Packet

Dear Members of the Board:

Enclosed, and with your permission, I submit my Parole Packet for your consideration.

Letters of support, educational and vocational accomplishment, parole plan, and other relative information for your consideration are provided within.

Thank you in advance for your consideration.

Very Respectfully,

Raymond E. Lumsden #1234567

w/encs

[SAMPLE]

PAROLE PACKET OF RAYMOND E. LUMSDEN
2109472

TABLE OF CONTENTS

(Page) #

Introduction Letter ....

Cover ....

Table of Contents ....

Educational & Vocational ....

Parole Plan ....

Resume ....

Support Letters ....

Employment Letters ....

Photos ....

Raymond E. Lumsden

[SAMPLE]

EDUCATIONAL & VOCATIONAL ACHIEVEMENTS

[SAMPLE]

PAROLE PLAN

1. Release:
   I originally planned to parole to my mother's home, Mrs. Lumsden, who lives at 1234 Alphabet Street, Dallas, Texas, 75201. My mother works as a nurse at Lakeside Hospital, and her phone number is 123-123-4567. She is financially capable and willing to offer support until I am able to secure employment and self-sustain.

2. Employment:
   I plan to become employed upon release at ABC Construction in Plano, Texas. Ronald McDonald is the manager willing to hire me; his number is 123-222-3333. His letter is included in this packet for review.

3. Goals:
   I have goals in place to ensure my success:

   Immediate- Arrive at parole, make an introduction with my assigned parole officer, enjoy dinner with my mother at my favorite restaurant, attend late service at my church.

   First Week- Report to my employer, acquire transportation, and enroll in AA classes.

   First Month- Begin making payments to parole and open an account to save for an apartment.

   First year: I successfully transitioned back into a normal life and purchased my own vehicle with insurance. I also established visitation with my children.

Raymond E. Lumsden

[SAMPLE]

RESUME

Food Preparation Cook
Hughes Unit- TDCJ
2010-2023

Prepared meals and assisted in cleaning the food service area.

McDonald's Restaurant
Houston, Texas
2008-2010\

Worked in all facets of food preparation.

Micheal's Steakhouse
Sanitation
2004-2008

Facilitated sanitation procedures.

Education:

2022, 150 hours of Authentic Manhood
2020, HVAC Certification at Hughes Unit
2009, GED Certification, Skyview Night School, Houston, Texas.

Skills

HVAC, Welding, Food Preparation, Sanitation.

[SAMPLE SUPPORT LETTER]

20, September, 2023

Texas Board of Pardons & Parole
P.O. Box 13401
Capital Station
Austin, Texas, 78711-3401

RE: Raymond E. Lumsden

Dear Board Members:

This letter is in support of my son, Raymond E. Lumsden, #1234567, who is currently located in the Hughes Unit.

Understandably, my views and support may come with a weaker recognition as the Mother, and since a certain level of bias may be attached, still, and in spite, there is not a person alive who knows Raymond better than I, his Mother, who raised him.

I make no excuses for Raymond's past behavior or the acts that caused his incarceration. More so, Raymond himself also accepts full blame and remorse for those actions. Trust me when I tell you that my Son is not today, the same person he was when he arrived at that prison so many years ago now.

Maturity, wisdom, and reformation have changed him back into the Son I have known all his life. For this, I am opening my home and resources to support his efforts to be introduced back into society, and successfully so. Whatever is necessary of me and from me will be his and for as long as is necessary for him to find his footing.

If there is anything that I can do to better his chances of release, please do not hesitate to call me. I appreciate your time and consideration.

Very Respectfully,

[Name/Address/Phone Number]

[SAMPLE EMPLOYMENT LETTER]

05, September, 2023

Texas Pardons and Parole
P.O. BOX 13401
Capital Station
Austin, Texas 78711-3401

RE: Letter of Employment for Raymond Lumsden

Dear Board Members;

My name is Ronald McDonald. I am the General Manager at McDonald Heating & Air in Dallas, Texas. My phone number is 214-222-2222.

I fully intend to employ Raymond Lumsden upon his release and have secured a position awaiting that date. If there is anything else I can do to assist in his review and parole, I stand ready and welcome your call.

Respectfully,

Ronald McDonald

Ronald McDonald 214-222-2222
12345 Johnson St.
Dallas, Texas, 75201

[SAMPLE PHOTOS]

As you can see from the Sample Parole Packet, it's not complicated in spite of my having simplified it as much as possible. All that demonstrates is that (1) you have initiative and care about your parole, and (2) it provides information about you, in your words, to the parole board for consideration.

Does it guarantee parole? Nope.
Does it really matter? 90% of board members say it does.

But, the truth is that you can still make parole without a parole packet, even in Texas, because the board does not require them in order to make parole. To be honest, you don't really *need* to do anything other than be parole-eligible.

You aren't required to submit anything; you aren't even required to attend your parole hearing if you do not want to. Support letters, certificates, and history are all totally unnecessary.

That being said, you're a damn fool if you don't.

Taking initiative and making an effort to be involved in your parole consideration is exactly the type of action that both the parole board and the citizens of your state want and expect from you. Stop the madness and prepare your parole packet *Today*.

And that doesn't mean flooding the parole board with calls, letters, and constant information. None of that is necessary, and it's far better to keep it simple as I have done in my Sample Parole Packet. As in all legal writings and prison-related issues, the rule is to *keep it short and simple.*

Yes, you can always and should hire a Parole Lawyer if you can, but from what information I received from a Texas Board Member, Mr. Brian Long, in preparation for this book, parole board members tend to look far more favorably on parole packets that the inmate prepares because it demonstrates initiative. They believe you should be considerate of the financial burden it places upon your family to pay for a parole lawyer because you are too lazy to prepare your own parole packet.

If *YOU*, the person wanting to be released to parole, are not prepared to take the initiative to put together your own packet even with the assistance of another inmate, then you are not of the preparedness for release to parole.

All those were Mr. Long's exact words.

He also pointed out some other information I will now address for my Texas inmates, specifically…

CHAPTER 4

TEXAS PAROLE: THE UNICORN

As the title chapter points out, parole in Texas is much like a Unicorn: Heard about but never seen. While the recent flurry of legislative action has improved the percentage of those granted parole, it is still no guarantee.

Here in Texas, the entire parole process is controlled by two parties: (1) The Texas Department of Criminal Justice and (2) The Texas Board of Pardons and Parole. When dealing with parole matters here, either of these agencies may be contacted.

Parole in Texas is merely a privilege and not a guaranteed right. Even if your prison record is squeaky clean, all of your parole programs are complete, and you are the perfect example of an inmate worthy of parole, *you can be denied.*

Do not take it personally; it happens to many every day.

The Texas Department of Criminal Justice—Parole Division identifies the inmates eligible for parole consideration approximately six months before their parole eligibility date. After that, and for subsequent parole review considerations, inmates are identified for parole consideration four months before their review date.

Once you are identified, the parole review commences, and all of your records, flies, and documents are gathered for review.

The first step is to be interviewed by a Unit Parole Officer here at the prison. During that brief and non-formal interview, they will review your prison file, release plan, contact information for your parole address, etc. Soon after, he will forward that information to the Parole Board for review to determine parole eligibility.

Always be courteous and respectful to the Unit Parole Officer. Their ideas, feelings, and input are highly regarded in the Parole Board's decision regarding your parole.

If and when you are being considered for parole, TDCJ will send a notice to the victim in your case, their family members, law enforcement involved in your case, etc. Anyone registered to receive notice on the Victim Notification System (VNS) will also receive notice of the parole review process and be provided the opportunity to protest you.

In fact, any victim defined and outlined by Texas Government Code 508.117 has the right to request a formal interview with the Texas Board of Pardons and Parole. No, as an inmate, you do not have a right to speak with or be brought before the Parole Board. Neither do your family or friends who support your parole.

Once the Parole Board has reached a decision related to your parole, you will be notified of that decision in writing in approximately 4-6 weeks.

There are Four (4) different types of parole in Texas:

- Parole
- Mandatory Supervision Release
- Discretionary Mandatory Supervision
- Discharge Release

1. *Parole*
   Here, your release is subject to your having to serve the remainder of your sentence under the direct supervision of a parole officer. If you are terminally ill or have extensive medical conditions, you may be eligible for Medically Recommended Intensive Supervision (MRIS). To qualify, you must be a nonviolent offender diagnosed with a terminal illness, either physically or mentally disabled, and pose no significant threat to the public.

   Under "MRIS," it is likely that you will be required to wear a tracking device, have a curfew, and follow very strict rules.

2. *Mandatory Supervision*
   Mandatory Supervision is released from prison implemented for criminal offenses committed on or after August 31, 1977. Now, and after September 1, 1996, It became purely discretionary.

3. *Discretionary Mandatory Supervision*
   For criminal offenses/convictions committed on or after September 1, 1996, the parole board is required under the law to vote on Discretionary Mandatory Supervision for those inmates whose good time, plus their actual time served, equals the term of their sentence.

   The Parole Board is required under the law to review those inmates who are eligible for Discretionary Mandatory Supervision on or before their eligibility date. If you are considered a danger to the public, or your accrued good conduct time is not an accurate description/reflection of your rehabilitative potential, the Board has the authority to deny you.

4. *Discharge Release*
   If you are not considered for parole or eligible, and have served your entire sentence day-for-day, you will be released without supervision or requirements. This isn't really

a type of "parole" but it is listed as such under Code.

I want to emphasize that if you are terminally ill, physically ill, mentally ill to the extent of being disabled, and are a non-violent offender who poses no risk to the safety of the public, I highly recommend that you apply for Medical Supervision.

Some refer to this as Compassionate Release.

Since 1991, inmate applicants have been screened by the Texas Correctional Office for Offenders with Medical or Mental Impairments (TCOOMMI) and Correctional Managed Health Care prior to being approved for Medical Supervision.

In order to be approved, and I stress this point, an inmate must be determined as no longer a threat to public safety and poses no risk of future offenses. The following do not qualify:

• Inmates with a 3g offense as described by Article 42.12 of the Texas Code of Criminal Procedure, unless they are found to be terminally ill or require long-term diagnosis;

• Non-citizens of the United States, unless being deported to another agency or country;

• Inmates are convicted under chapter 62 of the Texas Code of Criminal Procedure unless they are in a vegetative state or have total complete mobility loss.

Instead of telling you about the Texas Parole Eligibility Requirements, Good Time Earnings, and Parole Statistics, let me show you them as presented directly by the Texas Board of Pardons & Parole…

Classification	**Flat Time**	**Good Conduct Time Credit for completion of academic or vocation programs or on-the-job training**
Line Class 1 - Initial classification of new inmates	30 Days	Up to 15 Days for "A", "B", or "C" credits.
Line Class 2 - Inmates with disciplinary status	30 Days	Up to 15 Days for "A", "B", or "C" credits
Line Class 3 - Inmates with security custody. No good time credit earned.	30 Days	No Good Time Credit earned
Inmate on Parole or Mandatory Supervision – No good time credit can be earned.	30 Days	No Good Time Credit earned
While **confined in a county jail**	30 Days	Up to 20 Days
Supervision – No good time credit can be earned.		
While confined in a county jail	30 Days	Up to 15 Days for voluntary work program operated by the Sheriff

GOVERNMENT CODE

TITLE 4. EXECUTIVE BRANCH

SUBTITLE G. CORRECTIONS

CHAPTER 508. PAROLE AND MANDATORY SUPERVISION

SUBCHAPTER A. GENERAL PROVISIONS

Sec. 508.001. DEFINITIONS. In this chapter:

(1) "Board" means the Board of Pardons and Paroles.

(2) "Community supervision and corrections department" means a department established under Chapter 76.

(3) "Director" means the director of the pardons and paroles division.

(4) "Division" means the pardons and paroles division.

(5) "Mandatory supervision" means the release of an eligible inmate sentenced to the institutional division so that the inmate may serve the remainder of the inmate's sentence not on parole but under the supervision of the pardons and paroles division.

(6) "Parole" means the discretionary and conditional release of an eligible inmate sentenced to the institutional division so that the inmate may serve the remainder of the inmate's sentence under the supervision of the pardons and paroles division.

(7) "Parole officer" means a person appointed by the director and assigned the duties of assessment of risks and needs, investigation, case management, and supervision of releasees to ensure that releasees are complying with the conditions of parole or mandatory supervision.

(8) "Parole commissioner" means a person employed by the board to perform the duties described by Section 508.0441.

(9) "Releasee" means a person released on parole or to mandatory supervision.

(10) "Presiding officer" means the presiding officer of the Board of Pardons and Paroles.

Added by Acts 1997, 75th Leg., ch. 165, Sec. 12.01, eff. Sept. 1, 1997. Amended by Acts 1999, 76th Leg., ch. 62, Sec. 10.01, eff. Sept. 1, 1999; Acts 2003, 78th Leg., 3rd C.S., ch. 3, Sec. 11.02, eff. Jan. 11, 2004.

Sec. 508.002. CLEMENCY, COMMUTATION DISTINGUISHED. Neither parole nor mandatory supervision is a commutation of sentence or any other form of clemency.

Added by Acts 1997, 75th Leg., ch. 165, Sec. 12.01, eff. Sept. 1, 1997.

Sec. 508.003. INAPPLICABLE TO JUVENILES AND CERTAIN INMATES. (a) This chapter does not apply to an emergency absence under escort granted to an inmate by the institutional division under Section 501.006.

(b) Except as provided by Subsection (c), this chapter does not apply to release on parole from an institution for juveniles.

(c) The provisions of this chapter not in conflict with Section 508.156 apply to parole of a person from the Texas Juvenile Justice Department or from a post-adjudication secure correctional facility operated by or under contract with a juvenile board or local juvenile probation department under that section.

Added by Acts 1997, 75th Leg., ch. 165, Sec. 12.01, eff. Sept. 1, 1997.
Amended by:

Acts 2015, 84th Leg., R.S., Ch. 734 (H.B. 1549), Sec. 100, eff. September 1, 2015.

Acts 2015, 84th Leg., R.S., Ch. 854 (S.B. 1149), Sec. 6, eff. September 1, 2015.

SUBCHAPTER B. BOARD OF PARDONS AND PAROLES

Sec. 508.031. COMPOSITION OF BOARD. (a) The board consists of seven members appointed by the governor with the advice and consent of the senate.

(b) Appointments to the board must be made without regard to the race, color, disability, sex, religion, age, or national origin of the appointed members.

Added by Acts 1997, 75th Leg., ch. 165, Sec. 12.01, eff. Sept. 1, 1997. Amended by Acts 1999, 76th Leg., ch. 554, Sec. 1, eff. Sept. 1, 1999; Acts 2003, 78th Leg., 3rd C.S., ch. 3, Sec. 11.03, eff. Jan. 11, 2004.

Sec. 508.032. REQUIREMENTS FOR MEMBERSHIP. (a) Board members must be representative of the general public.

(b) A member must have resided in this state for the two years before appointment.

(c)(1) A person who is a former employee of the department may not serve on the board before the second anniversary of the date the person terminated employment with the department.

(2) A person who is employed by the department on August 1, 2003, may not serve on the board before August 1, 2005.

(d) At any time not more than three members of the board may be former employees of the department.

(e) For purposes of Subsections (c) and (d), previous service as a board member is not considered to be employment with the department.

Added by Acts 1997, 75th Leg., ch. 165, Sec. 12.01, eff. Sept. 1, 1997. Amended by Acts 2003, 78th Leg., 3rd C.S., ch. 3, Sec. 11.04, eff. Jan. 11, 2004.

Sec. 508.033. DISQUALIFICATIONS. (a) A person is not eligible for appointment as a member of the board or for employment as a parole commissioner if the person or the person's spouse:

(1) is employed by or participates in the management of a business entity or other organization receiving funds from the department or the board;

(2) owns or controls, directly or indirectly, more than a 10-percent interest in a business entity or other organization:

(A) regulated by the department; or

(B) receiving funds from the department or the board; or

(3) uses or receives a substantial amount of tangible goods, services, or funds from the department or the board, other than compensation or reimbursement authorized by law for board membership, attendance, or expenses.

(b) In determining eligibility under Subsection (a)(3), the compensation or reimbursement that a board member's spouse or parole commissioner's spouse receives as an employee of the board or the department may not be considered. This subsection does not affect any restriction on employment or board membership imposed by any other law.

(c) A person may not serve as a parole commissioner, may not be a member of the board, and may not be an employee of the division or the board employed in a "bona fide executive, administrative, or professional capacity," as that phrase is used for purposes of establishing an exemption to the overtime provisions of the federal Fair Labor Standards Act of 1938 (29 U.S.C. Section 201 et seq.) and its subsequent amendments, if:

(1) the person is an officer, employee, or paid consultant of a Texas trade association in the field of criminal justice; or

(2) the person's spouse is an officer, manager, or paid consultant of a Texas trade association in the field of criminal justice.

(d) A person who is required to register as a lobbyist under Chapter 305 because of the person's activities for compensation in or on behalf of a profession related to the operation of the board may not:

(1) serve as a member of the board or as a parole commissioner; or

(2) act as the general counsel to the board or division.

(e) In this section, "Texas trade association" means a cooperative and voluntarily joined association of business or professional competitors in this state designed to assist its members and its industry or profession in:

(1) dealing with mutual business or professional problems; and

(2) promoting their common interests.

(f) A person who is a current or former employee of the department may not serve as a parole commissioner before the second anniversary of the date the person's employment with the department ceases, and a member of the board may not serve as a parole commissioner before the second anniversary of the date the person's membership on the board ceases.

Added by Acts 1997, 75th Leg., ch. 165, Sec. 12.01, eff. Sept. 1, 1997.
Amended by Acts 1999, 76th Leg., ch. 62, Sec. 10.04, eff. Sept. 1, 1999; Acts 1999, 76th Leg., ch. 554, Sec. 2, eff. Sept. 1, 1999.
Amended by:

Acts 2007, 80th Leg., R.S., Ch. 1308 (S.B. 909), Sec. 33, eff. June 15, 2007.

Sec. 508.034. GROUNDS FOR REMOVAL. (a) It is a ground for removal from the board that a member:

(1) does not have at the time of taking office the qualification required by Section 508.032(b) for appointment to the board;

(2) is ineligible for membership under Section 508.033;

(3) is unable to discharge the member's duties for a substantial part of the term for which the member is appointed because of illness or disability; or

(4) is absent from more than half of the regularly scheduled board or panel meetings that the member is eligible to attend during each calendar year.

(b) The board administrator or the board administrator's designee shall provide to members of the board and to employees, as often as necessary, information regarding their qualification for office or employment under this chapter and their responsibilities under applicable laws relating to standards of conduct for state officers or employees.

(c) The validity of an action of the board or panel is not affected by the fact that the action is taken when a ground for removal of a board member exists.

(d) If the general counsel to the board has knowledge that a potential ground for removal exists, the general counsel shall notify the presiding officer of the board of the potential ground. The presiding officer shall notify the governor and the attorney general that a potential ground for removal exists. If the potential ground for removal involves the presiding officer, the general counsel to the board shall notify the governor and the attorney general that a potential ground for removal exists.

(e) It is a ground for removal from the board that a member fails to comply with policies or rules adopted by the board.

Added by Acts 1997, 75th Leg., ch. 165, Sec. 12.01, eff. Sept. 1, 1997. Amended by Acts 1999, 76th Leg., ch. 62, Sec. 10.05, eff. Sept. 1, 1999; Acts 1999, 76th Leg., ch. 554, Sec. 3, eff. Sept. 1, 1999; Acts 2001, 77th Leg., ch. 856, Sec. 1, eff. Sept. 1, 2001; Acts 2003, 78th Leg., 3rd C.S., ch. 3, Sec. 11.05, eff. Jan. 11, 2004.

Sec. 508.035. PRESIDING OFFICER. (a) The governor shall designate one member to serve as presiding officer of the board.

(b) The presiding officer serves in that capacity at the pleasure of the governor.

(c) The presiding officer reports directly to the governor and serves as the administrative head of the board.

(d) The presiding officer may:

(1) delegate responsibilities and authority to other members of the board, parole commissioners, or to employees of the board;

(2) appoint advisory committees from the membership of the board or from parole commissioners to further the efficient administration of board business; and

(3) establish policies and procedures to further the efficient administration of the business of the board.

Added by Acts 1997, 75th Leg., ch. 165, Sec. 12.01, eff. Sept. 1, 1997. Amended by Acts 2001, 77th Leg., ch. 856, Sec. 2, eff. Sept. 1, 2001; Acts 2003, 78th Leg., 3rd C.S., ch. 3, Sec. 11.06, eff. Jan. 11, 2004.

Sec. 508.036. GENERAL ADMINISTRATIVE DUTIES. (a) The presiding officer shall:

(1) develop and implement policies that clearly separate the policy-making responsibilities of the board and the management responsibilities of the board administrator, parole commissioners, and the staff of the board;

(2) establish caseloads and required work hours for members of the

board and parole commissioners;

(3) update parole guidelines, assign precedential value to previous decisions of the board relating to the granting of parole and the revocation of parole or mandatory supervision, and develop policies to ensure that members of the board and parole commissioners use guidelines and previous decisions of the board and parole commissioners in making decisions under this chapter;

(4) require members of the board and parole commissioners to file activity reports that provide information on release decisions made by members of the board and parole commissioners, the workload and hours worked of the members of the board and parole commissioners, and the use of parole guidelines by members of the board and parole commissioners; and

(5) report at least annually to the governor and the legislature on the activities of the board and parole commissioners, parole release decisions, and the use of parole guidelines by the board and parole commissioners.

(b) The board shall:

(1) adopt rules relating to the decision-making processes used by the board and parole panels;

(2) prepare information of public interest describing the functions of the board and make the information available to the public and appropriate state agencies;

(3) comply with federal and state laws related to program and facility accessibility; and

(4) develop and implement policies that provide the public with a reasonable opportunity to appear before the board and to speak on any issue under the jurisdiction of the board, with the exception of an individual parole determination or clemency recommendation.

(c) The board administrator shall prepare and maintain a written plan that describes how a person who does not speak English can be provided reasonable access to the board's programs and services.

(d) The board, in performing its duties, is subject to the open meetings law, Chapter 551, and the administrative procedure law, Chapter 2001. This subsection does not affect the provisions of Section 2001.223 exempting hearings and interviews conducted by the board or the division from Section 2001.038 and Subchapters C-H, Chapter 2001.

(e) The board, in accordance with the rules and procedures of the Legislative Budget Board, shall prepare, approve, and submit a legislative appropriations request that is separate from the legislative appropriations request for the department and is used to develop the board's budget structure. The board shall maintain the board's legislative appropriations request and budget structure separately from those of the department.

Added by Acts 1997, 75th Leg., ch. 165, Sec. 12.01, eff. Sept. 1, 1997. Amended by Acts 1999, 76th Leg., ch. 62, Sec. 10.06, eff. Sept. 1, 1999; Acts 2001, 77th Leg., ch. 856, Sec. 3, eff. Sept. 1, 2001; Acts 2003, 78th Leg., ch. 1170, Sec. 31.01, eff. Sept. 1, 2003; Acts 2003, 78th Leg., 3rd C.S., ch. 3, Sec. 11.07, eff. Jan. 11, 2004.

Amended by:

Acts 2007, 80th Leg., R.S., Ch. 1308 (S.B. 909), Sec. 34, eff. June 15, 2007.

Acts 2007, 80th Leg., R.S., Ch. 1308 (S.B. 909), Sec. 35, eff. June 15, 2007.

Acts 2011, 82nd Leg., R.S., Ch. 1083 (S.B. 1179), Sec. 9, eff. June 17, 2011.

Sec. 508.0362. TRAINING REQUIRED. (a) (1) A person who is appointed to and qualifies for office as a member of the board may not vote, deliberate, or be counted as a member in attendance at a meeting of the board until the person completes at least one course of a training program that complies with this section.

(2) A parole commissioner employed by the board may not vote or deliberate on a matter described by Section 508.0441 until the person completes at least one course of a training program that complies with this section.

(b) A training program must provide information to the person regarding:

(1) the enabling legislation that created the board;

(2) the programs operated by the board;

(3) the role and functions of the board and parole commissioners;

(4) the rules of the board;

(5) the current budget for the board;

(6) the results of the most recent formal audit of the board;

(7) the requirements of the:

(A) open meetings law, Chapter 551;

(B) open records law, Chapter 552; and

(C) administrative procedure law, Chapter 2001;

(8) the requirements of the conflict of interest laws and other laws relating to public officials; and

(9) any applicable ethics policies adopted by the board or the Texas Ethics Commission.

(c) A person appointed to the board is entitled to reimbursement, as provided by the General Appropriations Act, for the travel expenses incurred in attending the training program regardless of whether the attendance at the program occurs before or after the person qualifies for office.

Added by Acts 1999, 76th Leg., ch. 62, Sec. 10.08, eff. Sept. 1, 1999. Amended by Acts 1999, 76th Leg., ch. 554, Sec. 4, eff. Sept. 1, 1999; Acts 2003, 78th Leg., 3rd C.S., ch. 3, Sec. 11.08, eff. Jan. 11, 2004.

Sec. 508.037. TERMS; REMOVAL. (a) A board member holds office for a term of six years.

(b) The terms of one-third of the members expire February 1 of each odd-numbered year.

(c) The governor may remove a board member, other than a member appointed by another governor, at any time and for any reason.

Added by Acts 1997, 75th Leg., ch. 165, Sec. 12.01, eff. Sept. 1, 1997.

Sec. 508.038. VACANCIES. If a vacancy occurs, the governor shall appoint in the same manner as other appointments are made a person to serve the remainder of the unexpired term.

Added by Acts 1997, 75th Leg., ch. 165, Sec. 12.01, eff. Sept. 1, 1997.

Sec. 508.039. COMPENSATION. A board member is paid the salary the legislature determines in the General Appropriations Act.

Added by Acts 1997, 75th Leg., ch. 165, Sec. 12.01, eff. Sept. 1, 1997.

Sec. 508.040. PERSONNEL. (a) The presiding officer is responsible for the employment and supervision of:

(1) parole commissioners;

(2) a general counsel to the board;

(3) a board administrator to manage the day-to-day activities of the board;

(4) hearing officers;

(5) personnel to assist in clemency and hearing matters; and

(6) secretarial or clerical personnel.

(b) The board administrator or the board administrator's designee shall prepare and maintain a written policy statement that implements a program of equal employment opportunity under which all personnel decisions of the board are made without regard to race, color, disability, sex, religion, age, or national origin. The policy statement must include:

(1) personnel policies, including policies relating to recruitment, evaluation, selection, training, and promotion of personnel, that show the intent of the board to avoid the unlawful employment practices described by Chapter 21, Labor Code; and

(2) an analysis of the extent to which the composition of the board's personnel is in accordance with state and federal law and a description of reasonable methods to achieve compliance with state and federal law.

(c) The policy statement must be updated annually, be reviewed by the Commission on Human Rights for compliance with Subsection (b)(1), and be filed with the governor's office.

(d) The board administrator or the board administrator's designee shall develop an intra-agency career ladder program that addresses opportunities for mobility and advancement for employees within the board. The program shall require intra-agency posting of all positions concurrently with any public posting.

(e) The board administrator or the board administrator's designee shall develop a system of annual performance evaluations that are based on documented employee performance. All merit pay for board employees must be based on the system established under this subsection.

Added by Acts 1997, 75th Leg., ch. 165, Sec. 12.01, eff. Sept. 1, 1997. Amended by Acts 1999, 76th Leg., ch. 62, Sec. 10.09, eff. Sept. 1, 1999; Acts 1999, 76th Leg., ch. 554, Sec. 5, eff. Sept. 1, 1999; Acts 2003, 78th Leg., 3rd C.S., ch. 3, Sec. 11.09, eff. Jan. 11, 2004.

Sec. 508.041. DESIGNEE TRAINING; HANDBOOK. (a) The board shall develop and implement:

(1) a training program that each newly hired employee of the board designated to conduct hearings under Section 508.281 must complete before conducting a hearing without the assistance of a board member or experienced parole commissioner or designee; and

(2) a training program to provide an annual update to designees of the board on issues and procedures relating to the revocation process.

(b) The board shall prepare and biennially update a procedural manual to be used by designees of the board. The board shall include in the manual:

(1) descriptions of decisions in previous hearings determined by the board to have value as precedents for decisions in subsequent hearings;

(2) laws and court decisions relevant to decision making in hearings; and

(3) case studies useful in decision making in hearings.

(c) The board shall prepare and update as necessary a handbook to be made available to participants in hearings under Section 508.281, such as defense attorneys, persons released on parole or mandatory supervision, and witnesses. The handbook must describe in plain language the procedures used in a hearing under Section 508.281.

Added by Acts 1997, 75th Leg., ch. 165, Sec. 12.01, eff. Sept. 1, 1997. Amended by Acts 1999, 76th Leg., ch. 62, Sec. 10.10, eff. Sept. 1, 1999; Acts 2003, 78th Leg., 3rd C.S., ch. 3, Sec. 11.10, eff. Jan. 11, 2004.

Sec. 508.042. TRAINING PROGRAM FOR MEMBERS AND PAROLE COMMISSIONERS. (a) The board shall develop for board members and parole commissioners a comprehensive training and education program on the criminal justice system, with special emphasis on the parole process.

(b)(1) A new member may not participate in a vote of the board or a panel, deliberate, or be counted as a member in attendance at a meeting of the board until the member completes the program.

(2) A new parole commissioner may not participate in a vote of a panel until the commissioner completes the program. This subdivision does not apply to a new parole commissioner who as a board member completed the program.

Added by Acts 1997, 75th Leg., ch. 165, Sec. 12.01, eff. Sept. 1, 1997. Amended by Acts 1999, 76th Leg., ch. 62, Sec. 10.11, eff. Sept. 1, 1999; Acts 1999, 76th Leg., ch. 554, Sec. 6, eff. Sept. 1, 1999; Acts 2003, 78th Leg., 3rd C.S., ch. 3, Sec. 11.11, eff. Jan. 11, 2004.

Sec. 508.043. GIFTS AND GRANTS. The board may apply for and accept gifts or grants from any public or private source for use in any lawful purpose of the board.

Added by Acts 1997, 75th Leg., ch. 165, Sec. 12.01, eff. Sept. 1, 1997.

Sec. 508.044. POWERS AND DUTIES OF BOARD. A board member shall give full time to the duties of the member's office, including duties imposed on the board by the Texas Constitution and other law.

Added by Acts 1997, 75th Leg., ch. 165, Sec. 12.01, eff. Sept. 1, 1997. Amended by Acts 1999, 76th Leg., ch. 62, Sec. 10.12 to 10.14, eff. Sept. 1, 1999; Acts 2001, 77th Leg., ch. 856, Sec. 4, eff. Sept. 1, 2001; Acts 2003, 78th Leg., 3rd C.S., ch. 3, Sec. 11.12, eff. Jan. 11, 2004.

Sec. 508.0441. RELEASE AND REVOCATION DUTIES. (a) Board members and parole commissioners shall determine:

(1) which inmates are to be released on parole or mandatory supervision;

(2) conditions of parole or mandatory supervision, including special conditions;

(3) the modification and withdrawal of conditions of parole or mandatory supervision;

(4) which releasees may be released from supervision and reporting; and

(5) the continuation, modification, and revocation of parole or mandatory supervision.

(b) The board shall develop and implement a policy that clearly defines circumstances under which a board member or parole commissioner should disqualify himself or herself from voting on:

(1) a parole decision; or

(2) a decision to revoke parole or mandatory supervision.

(c) The board may adopt reasonable rules as proper or necessary relating to:

(1) the eligibility of an inmate for release on parole or release to mandatory supervision;

(2) the conduct of a parole or mandatory supervision hearing; or

(3) conditions to be imposed on a releasee.

(d) The presiding officer may provide a written plan for the administrative review of actions taken by a parole panel by a review panel.

(e) Board members and parole commissioners shall, at the direction of the presiding officer, file activity reports on duties performed under this chapter.

Added by Acts 1997, 75th Leg., ch. 165, Sec. 12.01, eff. Sept. 1, 1997. Amended by Acts 1999, 76th Leg., ch. 62, Sec. 10.12 to 10.14, eff. Sept. 1, 1999; Acts 2001, 77th Leg., ch. 856, Sec. 4, eff. Sept. 1, 2001. Redesignated from Government Code Sec. 508.044(b) to (f) and amended by Acts 2003, 78th Leg., 3rd C.S., ch. 3, Sec. 11.12, eff. Jan. 11, 2004.

Sec. 508.045. PAROLE PANELS. (a) Except as provided by Section 508.046, board members and parole commissioners shall act in panels composed of three in matters of:

(1) release on parole;

(2) release to mandatory supervision; and

(3) revocation of parole or mandatory supervision.

(b) The presiding officer shall designate the composition of each panel and shall designate panels composed of at least one board member and any combination of board members and parole commissioners.

(c) A parole panel may:

(1) grant, deny, or revoke parole;

(2) revoke mandatory supervision; and

(3) conduct parole revocation hearings and mandatory supervision revocation hearings.

Added by Acts 1997, 75th Leg., ch. 165, Sec. 12.01, eff. Sept. 1, 1997. Amended by Acts 2003, 78th Leg., 3rd C.S., ch. 3, Sec. 11.13, eff. Jan. 11, 2004.

Sec. 508.046. EXTRAORDINARY VOTE REQUIRED. To release on parole an inmate who was convicted of an offense under Section 20A.03, 21.02, 21.11(a)(1), or 22.021, Penal Code, or who is required under Section 508.145(c) to serve 35 calendar years before becoming eligible for release on parole, all members of the board must vote on the release on parole of the inmate, and at least two-thirds of the members must vote in favor of the release on parole. A member of the board may not vote on the release unless the member first receives a copy of a written report from the department on the probability that the inmate would commit an offense after being released on parole.

Added by Acts 1997, 75th Leg., ch. 165, Sec. 12.01, eff. Sept. 1, 1997.
Amended by:

Acts 2005, 79th Leg., Ch. 787 (S.B. 60), Sec. 3, eff. September 1, 2005.

Acts 2007, 80th Leg., R.S., Ch. 593 (H.B. 8), Sec. 3.38, eff. September 1, 2007.

Acts 2011, 82nd Leg., R.S., Ch. 122 (H.B. 3000), Sec. 9, eff. September 1, 2011.

Sec. 508.047. MEETINGS. (a) The members of the board shall meet at least once in each quarter of the calendar year at a site determined by the presiding officer.

(b) The members of the board are not required to meet as a body to perform the members' duties in clemency matters.

(c) A majority of each parole panel constitutes a quorum for the transaction of the panel's business. A panel's decision must be by majority vote.

(d) The members of a parole panel are not required to meet as a body to perform the members' duties, except to conduct a hearing under Section 508.281.

Added by Acts 1997, 75th Leg., ch. 165, Sec. 12.01, eff. Sept. 1, 1997. Amended by Acts 1999, 76th Leg., ch. 62, Sec. 10.15, eff. Sept. 1, 1999; Acts 2003, 78th Leg., 3rd C.S., ch. 3, Sec. 11.14, eff. Jan. 11, 2004.

Sec. 508.048. SUBPOENAS. (a) A parole panel may issue a subpoena requiring the attendance of a witness or the production of any record, book, paper, or document the panel considers necessary for investigation of the case of a person before the panel.

(b) A member of the board may sign a subpoena and administer an oath.

(c) A peace officer, parole officer, or community supervision and corrections department officer may serve the subpoena in the same manner as similar process in a court of record having original jurisdiction of criminal actions is served.

(d) A person who testifies falsely, fails to appear when subpoenaed, or fails or refuses to produce material under the subpoena is subject to the same orders and penalties to which a person taking those actions before a court is subject.

(e) On application of the board, a court of record having original jurisdiction of criminal actions may compel the attendance of a witness, the production of material, or the giving of testimony before the board, by an attachment for contempt or in the same manner as the court may otherwise compel the production of evidence.

Added by Acts 1997, 75th Leg., ch. 165, Sec. 12.01, eff. Sept. 1, 1997.

Sec. 508.0481. VICTIM'S RIGHT TO REPRESENTATION. (a) If a victim, close relative of a deceased victim, or guardian of a victim is required by a subpoena issued under Section 508.048 to appear at a hearing, the victim, relative, or guardian is entitled to representation by counsel at the hearing.

(b) This section does not require the state to provide representation by counsel to a victim, close relative of a deceased victim, or guardian of a victim.

(c) In this section, "victim," "close relative of a deceased victim," and "guardian of a victim" have the meanings assigned by Section 508.117.

Added by Acts 2001, 77th Leg., ch. 1034, Sec. 10, eff. Sept. 1, 2001.

Sec. 508.049. MISSION STATEMENT. (a) The board, after consultation with the governor and the Texas Board of Criminal Justice, shall adopt a mission statement that reflects the responsibilities for the operation of the parole process that are assigned to the board, the division, the department, or the Texas Board of Criminal Justice.

(b) The board shall include in the mission statement a description of specific locations at which the board intends to conduct business related to the operation of the parole process.

Added by Acts 1997, 75th Leg., ch. 165, Sec. 12.01, eff. Sept. 1, 1997. Amended by Acts 1999, 76th Leg., ch. 62, Sec. 10.16, eff. Sept. 1, 1999; Acts 2003, 78th Leg., 3rd C.S., ch. 3, Sec. 11.15, eff. Jan. 11, 2004.

Sec. 508.050. REPORT TO GOVERNOR. (a) On request of the governor, the board shall investigate a person being considered by the governor for:

(1) pardon;

(2) commutation of sentence;

(3) reprieve;

(4) remission of fine; or

(5) forfeiture.

(b) The board shall report to the governor on its investigation and make recommendations about the person to the governor.

Added by Acts 1997, 75th Leg., ch. 165, Sec. 12.01, eff. Sept. 1, 1997.

Sec. 508.051. SUNSET PROVISION. The Board of Pardons and Paroles is subject to review under Chapter 325 (Texas Sunset Act), but is not abolished under that chapter. The board shall be reviewed during the period in which the Texas Department of Criminal Justice is reviewed.

Added by Acts 1997, 75th Leg., ch. 165, Sec. 12.01, eff. Sept. 1, 1997. Amended by Acts 1999, 76th Leg., ch. 62, Sec. 10.17, eff. Sept. 1, 1999.

Sec. 508.052. COMPUTERS; OFFICE SPACE; OTHER EQUIPMENT. (a) The department by interagency contract may provide to the board necessary computer equipment and computer access to all computerized records and physical access to all printed records in the custody of the department that are related to the duties and functions of the board.

(b) The department by interagency contract may provide to the board necessary and appropriate:

(1) office space at locations designated by the presiding officer of the board; and

(2) utilities and communications equipment.

Added by Acts 1997, 75th Leg., ch. 165, Sec. 12.01, eff. Sept. 1, 1997.

Sec. 508.053. USE OF TECHNOLOGY. The board shall implement a policy requiring the board to use appropriate technological solutions to improve the board's ability to perform its functions. The policy must ensure that the public is able to interact with the board on the Internet.

Added by Acts 2007, 80th Leg., R.S., Ch. 1308 (S.B. 909), Sec. 36, eff. June 15, 2007.

Sec. 508.054. RECORDS OF COMPLAINTS. (a) The board shall maintain a system to promptly and efficiently act on complaints filed with the board. The board shall maintain information about parties to the complaint, the subject matter of the complaint, a summary of the results of the review or investigation of the complaint, and its disposition.

(b) The board shall make information available describing its procedures for complaint investigation and resolution.

(c) The board shall periodically notify the complaint parties of the status of the complaint until final disposition.

(d) This section does not apply to a complaint about an individual parole determination or clemency recommendation.

Added by Acts 2007, 80th Leg., R.S., Ch. 1308 (S.B. 909), Sec. 36, eff. June 15, 2007.

Sec. 508.055. NEGOTIATED RULEMAKING AND ALTERNATIVE DISPUTE RESOLUTION. (a) The board shall develop and implement a policy to encourage the use of:

(1) negotiated rulemaking procedures under Chapter 2008 for the adoption of board rules; and

(2) appropriate alternative dispute resolution procedures under Chapter 2009 to assist in the resolution of internal disputes under the board's jurisdiction.

(b) The board's procedures relating to alternative dispute resolution must conform, to the extent possible, to any model guidelines issued by the State Office of Administrative Hearings for the use of alternative dispute resolution by state agencies.

(c) The board shall designate a trained person to:

(1) coordinate the implementation of the policy adopted under Subsection (a);

(2) serve as a resource for any training needed to implement the procedures for negotiated rulemaking or alternative dispute resolution; and

(3) collect data concerning the effectiveness of those procedures, as implemented by the board.

Added by Acts 2007, 80th Leg., R.S., Ch. 1308 (S.B. 909), Sec. 36, eff. June 15, 2007.

SUBCHAPTER C. REPRESENTATION OF INMATES

Sec. 508.081. DEFINITIONS. In this subchapter:

(1) "Compensation" has the meaning assigned by Section 305.002.

(2) "Inmate" includes:

(A) an administrative releasee;

(B) an inmate imprisoned in the institutional division; and

(C) a person confined in a county jail awaiting:

(i) transfer to the institutional division; or

(ii) a revocation hearing.

(3) "Represent" means to directly or indirectly contact in person or by telephone, facsimile transmission, or correspondence a member or employee of the board or an employee of the department on behalf of an inmate.

Added by Acts 1997, 75th Leg., ch. 165, Sec. 12.01, eff. Sept. 1, 1997.
Amended by:

Acts 2021, 87th Leg., R.S., Ch. 126 (H.B. 719), Sec. 7, eff. September 1, 2021.

Sec. 508.082. RULES. The board shall adopt rules relating to:

(1) the submission and presentation of information and arguments to the board, a parole panel, and the department for and in behalf of an inmate; and

(2) the time, place, and manner of contact between a person representing an inmate and:

(A) a member of the board or a parole commissioner;

(B) an employee of the board; or

(C) an employee of the department.

Added by Acts 1997, 75th Leg., ch. 165, Sec. 12.01, eff. Sept. 1, 1997.
Amended by Acts 1999, 76th Leg., ch. 62, Sec. 10.18, eff. Sept. 1, 1999; Acts 2003, 78th Leg., 3rd C.S., ch. 3, Sec. 11.16, eff. Jan. 11, 2004.

Sec. 508.083. ELIGIBILITY TO REPRESENT INMATES. (a) A person who represents an inmate for compensation must:

(1) be an attorney licensed in this state; and

(2) register with the division.

(b) A person serving as a member or employee of the board or the Texas Board of Criminal Justice may not, before the second anniversary of the date the person ceases to be a board member or employee:

(1) represent any person in a matter before the board or a parole panel; or

(2) receive compensation for services rendered on behalf of any person regarding a matter pending before the board or a parole panel.

(c) A person, other than a person subject to Subsection (b), who is employed by the department may not, before the second anniversary of the date the person terminates service with the department:

(1) represent an inmate in a matter before the board or a parole panel; or

(2) receive compensation for services rendered on behalf of any person regarding a matter pending before the board or a parole panel.

(d) Repealed by Acts 2003, 78th Leg., ch 1007, Sec. 2.

Added by Acts 1997, 75th Leg., ch. 165, Sec. 12.01, eff. Sept. 1, 1997.
Amended by Acts 2003, 78th Leg., ch. 1007, Sec. 1, 2, eff. Sept. 1, 2003.

Sec. 508.084. FEE AFFIDAVIT. (a) A person required to register under Section 508.083, before the person first contacts a member of the board, an employee of the board, or an employee of the department on behalf of an inmate, shall file a fee affidavit with the department in a form prescribed by the department for each inmate the person represents for compensation.

(b) The fee affidavit must be written and verified and contain a statement of:

(1) the registrant's full name and address;

(2) the registrant's normal business, business phone number, and business address;

(3) the full name of any former member or employee of the board or the Texas Board of Criminal Justice or any former employee of the department with whom the registrant:

(A) is associated;

(B) has a relationship as an employer or employee; or

(C) maintains a contractual relationship to provide services;

(4) the full name and institutional identification number of the inmate the registrant represents;

(5) the amount of compensation the registrant has received or

expects to receive in exchange for the representation; and

(6) the name of the person providing the compensation.

(c) If a registrant receives compensation in excess of the amount reported on the fee affidavit, the registrant shall file with the department, not later than the fifth day after the date the registrant receives compensation in excess of the reported amount, a supplemental fee affidavit in a form prescribed by the department indicating the total amount of compensation received for representing the inmate.

(d) For each fee affidavit and supplemental fee affidavit received, the department shall:

(1) keep a copy of the affidavit in a central location; and

(2) not later than the third day after the date the affidavit is filed, place a copy of the affidavit in the inmate's file that is reviewed by a parole panel or the board.

Added by Acts 1997, 75th Leg., ch. 165, Sec. 12.01, eff. Sept. 1, 1997.

Sec. 508.085. REPRESENTATION SUMMARY FORM. (a) A person required to register under Section 508.083 shall, for each calendar year in which the person represents an inmate, file a representation summary form with the division on a form prescribed by the division.

(b) The form must be filed not later than January 31 of the year succeeding the year for which the report is filed and must include a statement of:

(1) the registrant's full name and address;

(2) the registrant's normal business, business phone number, and business address;

(3) the full name of any former member or employee of the board or the Texas Board of Criminal Justice or any former employee of the department with whom the registrant:

(A) is associated;

(B) has a relationship as an employer or employee; or

(C) maintains a contractual relationship to provide services;

(4) the full name and institutional identification number of each inmate the registrant represented in the previous calendar year; and

(5) the amount of compensation the registrant has received for representing each inmate in the previous calendar year.

(c) A person who files a form under this section and for whom the information required for the form has changed shall, not later than the 10th day after the date the information changes, file a supplemental statement with the division indicating the change.

Added by Acts 1997, 75th Leg., ch. 165, Sec. 12.01, eff. Sept. 1, 1997.

Sec. 508.086. CRIMINAL PENALTIES. (a) A former member or employee of the board or the Texas Board of Criminal Justice or a former employee of the department commits an offense if the former member or employee violates Section 508.083(b), (c), or (d).

(b) A person who represents an inmate for compensation commits an offense if the person is not an attorney licensed in this state.

(c) A person who is required to file an affidavit under Section 508.084(a) or (c) or a form or statement under Section 508.085 commits an offense if the person fails to file the affidavit, form, or statement.

(d) An offense under Subsection (a) is a Class A misdemeanor. An offense under Subsection (b) or (c) is a Class C misdemeanor.

Added by Acts 1997, 75th Leg., ch. 165, Sec. 12.01, eff. Sept. 1, 1997.

SUBCHAPTER D. PARDONS AND PAROLES DIVISION

Sec. 508.111. DIRECTOR. (a) The executive director shall hire the director of the division.

(b) The director is responsible for the administration of the division.

Added by Acts 1997, 75th Leg., ch. 165, Sec. 12.01, eff. Sept. 1, 1997.

Sec. 508.112. DUTY OF DIVISION. The division is responsible for the investigation and supervision of all releasees.

Added by Acts 1997, 75th Leg., ch. 165, Sec. 12.01, eff. Sept. 1, 1997.

Sec. 508.113. PAROLE OFFICERS, SUPERVISORS: QUALIFICATIONS. (a) This subsection and Subsection (b) apply only to a person employed as a parole officer or supervisor on or before September 1, 1990. A person may not be employed as a parole officer or supervisor, or be responsible for investigating or supervising a releasee, unless the person has:

(1) four years of successfully completed education in an accredited college or university;

(2) two years of full-time paid employment in responsible correctional work with adults or juveniles or in a related field; and

(3) any other qualifications that may be specified by the director.

(b) Additional experience in a category described by Subsection (a)(2) may be substituted year for year for the required college education, with a maximum substitution of two years.

(c) The director shall establish qualifications for parole officers and supervisors that are the same as qualifications for community supervision and corrections department officers imposed by Section 76.005. A person may not begin employment as a parole officer or supervisor after September 1, 1990, unless the person meets the qualifications established by the director.

(d) A person who is serving as a peace officer or as a prosecuting attorney may not act as a parole officer or be responsible for supervising a releasee.

Added by Acts 1997, 75th Leg., ch. 165, Sec. 12.01, eff. Sept. 1, 1997.

Sec. 508.1131. SALARY CAREER LADDER FOR PAROLE OFFICERS. (a) The executive director shall adopt a salary career ladder for parole officers. The salary career ladder must base a parole officer's salary on the officer's classification and years of service with the department.

(b) For purposes of the salary schedule, the department shall classify all parole officer positions as Parole Officer I, Parole Officer II, Parole Officer III, Parole Officer IV, or Parole Officer V.

(c) Under the salary career ladder adopted under Subsection (a), a parole officer to whom the schedule applies and who received an overall evaluation of at least satisfactory in the officer's most recent annual evaluation is entitled to an annual salary increase, during each of the officer's first 10 years of service in a designated parole officer classification as described by Subsection (b), equal to one-tenth of the difference between:

(1) the officer's current annual salary; and

(2) the minimum annual salary of a parole officer in the next highest classification.

Added by Acts 2007, 80th Leg., R.S., Ch. 1308 (S.B. 909), Sec. 37, eff. June 15, 2007.

Sec. 508.114. PAROLE OFFICERS, SUPERVISORS: ADDITIONAL DUTIES. (a) The judge of a court having original jurisdiction of criminal actions may, with the approval of the director, designate a parole officer or supervisor as a community supervision and corrections department officer. The director must give prior written approval for the payment of a proportional part of the salary paid to the parole officer or supervisor in compensation for service as a community supervision and corrections department officer. The director shall periodically report to the governor and the legislature the proportional salary payments.

(b) A parole officer or supervisor, on request of the governor or on order of the director, shall be responsible for supervising an inmate placed on conditional pardon or granted an emergency absence under escort.

Added by Acts 1997, 75th Leg., ch. 165, Sec. 12.01, eff. Sept. 1, 1997.

Sec. 508.1141. SPECIALIZED TRAINING; GANG MEMBERS. The department shall develop and provide specialized training for parole officers supervising releasees previously identified by the department as being members of prison gangs, criminal street gangs, or security threat groups.

Added by Acts 1999, 76th Leg., ch. 490, Sec. 1, eff. Sept. 1, 1999.

Sec. 508.1142. PAROLE OFFICER MAXIMUM CASELOADS. (a) The department shall adopt a policy that establishes guidelines for a maximum caseload for each parole officer of:

(1) 60 active releasees, if the releasees are not in a specialized program described by Subdivisions (2)-(6);

(2) 35 active releasees, if the releasees are in the special needs offender program;

(3) 35 active releasees, if the releasees are in the therapeutic community substance abuse aftercare treatment program;

(4) 24 active releasees, if the releasees are in the sex offender program;

(5) 20 active releasees, if the releasees are electronically monitored; and

(6) 11 active releasees, if the releasees are in the super-intensive supervision program.

(b) If the department is unable to meet the maximum caseload guidelines, the department shall submit a report to the Legislative Budget Board, at the end of each fiscal year in which the department fails to meet the guidelines, stating the amount of money needed by the department to meet the guidelines.

Added by Acts 2007, 80th Leg., R.S., Ch. 1421 (H.B. 3736), Sec. 1, eff. June 15, 2007.

Sec. 508.115. NOTIFICATION OF RELEASE OF INMATE. (a) Not later than the 11th day before the date a parole panel orders the release on parole of an inmate or not later than the 11th day after the date the board recommends that the governor grant executive clemency, the division shall notify the sheriffs, each chief of police, the prosecuting attorneys, and the district judges in the county in which the inmate was convicted and the county to which the inmate is released that a parole panel is considering release on parole or the governor is considering clemency.

(b) In a case in which there was a change of venue, the division shall notify the sheriff, the prosecuting attorney, and the district judge in the county in which the prosecution was originated if, not later than the 30th day after the date the inmate was sentenced, those officials request in writing that the division give the officials notice under this section of a release of the inmate.

(c) Not later than the 10th day after the date a parole panel orders the transfer of an inmate to a halfway house under this chapter, the division shall give notice in accordance with Subsection (d) to:

(1) the sheriff of the county in which the inmate was convicted;

(2) the sheriff of the county in which the halfway house is located and each chief of police in the county; and

(3) the attorney who represents the state in the prosecution of felonies in the county in which the halfway house is located.

(d) The notice must state:

(1) the inmate's name;

(2) the county in which the inmate was convicted; and

(3) the offense for which the inmate was convicted.

(e) The notice must be provided by e-mail or other electronic communication.

Added by Acts 1997, 75th Leg., ch. 165, Sec. 12.01, eff. Sept. 1, 1997. Amended by Acts 1999, 76th Leg., ch. 62, Sec. 10.19, eff. Sept. 1, 1999; Acts 2001, 77th Leg., ch. 856, Sec. 5, eff. Sept. 1, 2001.
Amended by:
Acts 2011, 82nd Leg., R.S., Ch. 1123 (H.B. 200), Sec. 5, eff. September 1, 2011.

Sec. 508.116. PAROLE INFORMATION PROGRAM. (a) The division shall develop and implement a comprehensive program to inform inmates, the inmates' families, and other interested parties about the parole process.

(b) The division shall update the program annually.

Added by Acts 1997, 75th Leg., ch. 165, Sec. 12.01, eff. Sept. 1, 1997.

Sec. 508.117. VICTIM NOTIFICATION. (a) Before a parole panel considers for release on parole an inmate who is serving a sentence for an offense in which a person was a victim, the division, using the name and address provided on the victim impact statement, shall make a reasonable effort to notify:

(1) the victim;

(2) if the victim has a guardian, the guardian; or

(3) if the victim is deceased, a close relative of the deceased victim.

(b) A victim, guardian of a victim, or close relative of a deceased victim who would have been entitled to notification of parole consideration by the division but failed to provide a victim impact statement containing the person's name and address may file with the division a written request for notification. After receiving the written request, the division shall grant to the person all privileges, including notification under this section, to which the person would have been entitled had the person submitted a completed victim impact statement.

(c) If the notice is sent to a guardian or close relative of a deceased victim, the notice must contain a request by the division that the guardian or relative inform other persons having an interest in the matter that the inmate is being considered for release on parole.

(d) The failure of the division to comply with notice requirements of this section is not a ground for revocation of parole.

(e) Before an inmate is released from the institutional division on parole or to mandatory supervision, the pardons and paroles division shall give notice of the release to a person entitled to notification of parole consideration for the inmate under Subsection (a) or (b).

(f) Except as necessary to comply with this section, the board or the department may not disclose to any person the name or address of a person entitled to notice under this section unless:

(1) the person approves the disclosure; or

(2) a court determines that there is good cause for disclosure and orders the board or the department to disclose the information.

(g) In this section:

(1) "Close relative of a deceased victim" means a person who was:

(A) the spouse of the victim at the time of the victim's death;

(B) a parent of the deceased victim;

(C) an adult brother, sister, or child of the deceased victim; or

(D) the nearest relative of the deceased victim by consanguinity, if the persons described by Paragraphs (A) through (C) are deceased or are incapacitated due to physical or mental illness or infirmity.

(2) "Guardian of a victim" means a person who is the legal guardian of a victim, whether or not the legal relationship between the guardian and

the victim exists because of the age of the victim or the physical or mental incompetency of the victim.

(2-a) "Sexual assault" includes an offense under Section 21.02, Penal Code.

(3) "Victim" means a person who:

(A) is a victim of sexual assault, kidnapping, aggravated robbery, or felony stalking; or

(B) has suffered bodily injury or death as the result of the criminal conduct of another.

Added by Acts 1997, 75th Leg., ch. 165, Sec. 12.01, eff. Sept. 1, 1997.
Amended by:

Acts 2007, 80th Leg., R.S., Ch. 593 (H.B. 8), Sec. 3.39, eff. September 1, 2007.

Acts 2007, 80th Leg., R.S., Ch. 826 (H.B. 309), Sec. 1, eff. June 15, 2007.

Acts 2007, 80th Leg., R.S., Ch. 1308 (S.B. 909), Sec. 38, eff. June 15, 2007.

Sec. 508.118. HALFWAY HOUSES. (a) The division, in conjunction with the institutional division, shall use halfway houses to divert from housing in regular units of the institutional division suitable low-risk inmates and other inmates who would benefit from a smoother transition from incarceration to supervised release.

(b) Before transferring an inmate to a halfway house, the division shall send to the director of the halfway house all information relating to the inmate that the division determines will aid the halfway house in helping the inmate make a transition from the institutional division to supervised release.

(c) The division is responsible for supervising an inmate:

(1) for whom a presumptive parole date has been established; and

(2) who is transferred into a preparole residence in a halfway house under Subchapter A, Chapter 499.

Added by Acts 1997, 75th Leg., ch. 165, Sec. 12.01, eff. Sept. 1, 1997.

Sec. 508.119. COMMUNITY RESIDENTIAL FACILITIES. (a) The purpose of a community residential facility is to provide housing, supervision, counseling, personal, social, and work adjustment training, and other programs to:

(1) releasees who are required by a parole panel as a condition of release on parole or to mandatory supervision to serve a period in a community

residential facility; and

(2) releasees whose parole or mandatory supervision has been continued or modified under Section 508.283 and on whom sanctions have been imposed under that section.

(b) The division may establish and operate, or contract for the operation of, community residential facilities.

(c) The division may contract with a public or private vendor for the financing, construction, operation, or management of a community residential facility using a lease-purchase or installment sale contract to provide or supplement housing, board, or supervision for releasees placed in a community residential facility. A releasee housed or supervised in a facility operated by a vendor under a contract is subject to the same laws as if the housing or supervision were provided directly by the division.

(d) Unless the division or a vendor proposing to operate a community residential facility provides notice of a following proposed action and a hearing on the issues in the same manner as required under Section 509.010, the division may not:

(1) establish or contract for a community residential facility;

(2) change the use of a community residential facility;

(3) significantly increase the capacity of a community residential facility; or

(4) increase the capacity of a community residential facility to more than 500 residents, regardless of whether the increase is significant.

(e) Subsection (d) applies to any residential facility that the division establishes or contracts for under:

(1) this chapter;

(2) Subchapter C, Chapter 497; or

(3) Subchapter A, Chapter 499.

(f) The Texas Board of Criminal Justice shall adopt rules necessary for the management of a community residential facility.

(g) The division may charge to a releasee housed in a community residential facility a reasonable fee for the cost of housing, board, and the part of the administrative costs of the facility that is properly allocable to the releasee. The fee may not exceed the actual costs to the division for services to that releasee. The division may not deny placement in a community residential facility to a releasee because the releasee is unable to pay the fee.

(h) A parole panel or a designated agent of the division may grant a limited release to a releasee placed in a community residential facility to maintain or seek employment or participation in an education or training course or to seek housing after release from the facility.

(i) The notice required by Subsection (d) must clearly state that the proposed action concerns a facility in which persons who have been released from prison on parole or to mandatory supervision are to be housed.

Added by Acts 1997, 75th Leg., ch. 165, Sec. 12.01, eff. Sept. 1, 1997. Amended by Acts 1999, 76th Leg., ch. 62, Sec. 10.20, eff. Sept. 1, 1999.

SUBCHAPTER E. PAROLE AND MANDATORY SUPERVISION; RELEASE PROCEDURES

Sec. 508.141. AUTHORITY TO CONSIDER AND ORDER RELEASE ON PAROLE. (a) A parole panel may consider for release and release on parole an inmate who:

(1) has been sentenced to a term of imprisonment in the institutional division;

(2) is confined in a penal or correctional institution, including a jail in this state, a federal correctional institution, or a jail or a correctional institution in another state; and

(3) is eligible for release on parole.

(b) A parole is issued only on the order of a parole panel.

(c) Before releasing an inmate on parole, a parole panel may have the inmate appear before the panel and interview the inmate.

(d) A parole panel may release an inmate on parole during the parole month established for the inmate if the panel determines that the inmate's release will not increase the likelihood of harm to the public.

(e) A parole panel may release an inmate on parole only when:

(1) arrangements have been made for the inmate's employment or for the inmate's maintenance and care, which may include the issuance of payment for the cost of temporary post-release housing under Section 508.157; and

(2) the parole panel believes that the inmate is able and willing to fulfill the obligations of a law-abiding citizen.

(f) A parole panel may order a parole only for the best interest of society and not as an award of clemency.

(g) The board shall adopt a policy establishing the date on which the board may reconsider for release an inmate who has previously been denied release. The policy must require the board to reconsider for release:

(1) an inmate serving a sentence for an offense listed in Section 508.149(a) or for an offense punishable as a felony of the second or third degree under Section 22.04, Penal Code, during a month designated under Subsection (g-1) by the parole panel that denied release; and

(2) an inmate other than an inmate described by Subdivision (1) as soon as practicable after the first anniversary of the date of the denial.

(g-1) The month designated under Subsection (g)(1) by the parole panel that denied release must begin after the first anniversary of the date of the denial and end before the fifth anniversary of the date of the denial, unless the inmate is serving a sentence for an offense under Section 22.021, Penal Code, or a life sentence for a capital felony, in which event the designated month must begin after the first anniversary of the date of the denial and end before the 10th anniversary of the date of the denial.

Added by Acts 1997, 75th Leg., ch. 165, Sec. 12.01, eff. Sept. 1, 1997. Amended by Acts 2003, 78th Leg., ch. 349, Sec. 1, eff. June 18, 2003; Acts 2003, 78th Leg., 3rd C.S., ch. 3, Sec. 11.17, eff. Jan. 11, 2004.
Amended by:

Acts 2009, 81st Leg., R.S., Ch. 944 (H.B. 3226), Sec. 2, eff. June 19, 2009.

Acts 2013, 83rd Leg., R.S., Ch. 1256 (H.B. 431), Sec. 2, eff. June 14, 2013.

Acts 2015, 84th Leg., R.S., Ch. 358 (H.B. 1914), Sec. 1, eff. September 1, 2015.

Sec. 508.1411. NOTIFICATION OF PAROLE PANEL DECISION. (a) For each decision of a parole panel granting or denying the release of an inmate on parole, or denying the release of an inmate on mandatory supervision, the parole panel shall:

(1) produce a written statement, in clear and understandable language, that explains:

(A) the decision; and

(B) the reasons for the decision only to the extent those reasons relate specifically to the inmate;

(2) provide a copy of the statement to the inmate; and

(3) place a copy of the statement in the inmate's file.

(b) In a written statement produced under Subsection (a), the parole panel may withhold information that:

(1) is confidential and not subject to public disclosure under Chapter 552; or

(2) the parole panel considers to possibly jeopardize the health or safety of any individual.

(c) The board shall keep a copy of each statement produced under Subsection (a) in a central location.

Added by Acts 2013, 83rd Leg., R.S., Ch. 1154 (S.B. 213), Sec. 14, eff. September 1, 2013.

Sec. 508.142. PERIOD OF PAROLE. (a) The institutional division shall provide the board with sentence time credit information for each inmate who is eligible for release on parole.

(b) Good conduct time credit is computed for an inmate as if the inmate were confined in the institutional division during the entire time the inmate was actually confined.

(c) The period of parole is computed by subtracting from the term for which the inmate was sentenced the calendar time served on the sentence.

Added by Acts 1997, 75th Leg., ch. 165, Sec. 12.01, eff. Sept. 1, 1997.

Sec. 508.143. LEGAL CUSTODY OF RELEASEE. (a) A releasee while on parole is in the legal custody of the division.

(b) A releasee while on mandatory supervision is in the legal custody of the state.

Added by Acts 1997, 75th Leg., ch. 165, Sec. 12.01, eff. Sept. 1, 1997.

Sec. 508.144. PAROLE GUIDELINES AND RANGE OF RECOMMENDED PAROLE APPROVAL RATES. (a) The board shall:

(1) develop according to an acceptable research method the parole guidelines that are the basic criteria on which a parole decision is made;

(2) base the guidelines on the seriousness of the offense and the likelihood of a favorable parole outcome;

(3) ensure that the guidelines require consideration of an inmate's progress in any programs in which the inmate participated during the inmate's term of confinement;

(4) establish and maintain a range of recommended parole approval rates for each category or score within the guidelines; and

(5) implement the guidelines.

(b) The board shall meet annually to review and discuss the parole guidelines and range of recommended parole approval rates. The board may consult outside experts to assist with the review. The board shall prioritize the use of outside experts, technical assistance, and training in taking any action under Subsection (c). The board must consider:

(1) how the parole guidelines and range of recommended parole approval rates serve the needs of parole decision-making; and

(2) the extent to which the parole guidelines and range of recommended parole approval rates reflect parole panel decisions and predict successful parole outcomes.

(c) Based on the board's review under Subsection (b), the board may:

(1) update the guidelines by:

(A) including new risk factors; or

(B) changing the values of offense severity or risk factor scores; or

(2) modify the range of recommended parole approval rates under the guidelines, if parole approval rates differ significantly from the range of recommended parole approval rates.

(d) The board is not required to hold an open meeting to review the parole guidelines and range of recommended parole approval rates as required by Subsection (b), but any modifications or updates to the guidelines or range of recommended parole approval rates made by the board under Subsection (c) must occur in an open meeting.

Added by Acts 1997, 75th Leg., ch. 165, Sec. 12.01, eff. Sept. 1, 1997.
Amended by Acts 2003, 78th Leg., 3rd C.S., ch. 3, Sec. 11.18, eff. Jan. 11, 2004.
Amended by:

Acts 2007, 80th Leg., R.S., Ch. 1308 (S.B. 909), Sec. 39, eff. June 15, 2007.

Acts 2013, 83rd Leg., R.S., Ch. 1154 (S.B. 213), Sec. 15, eff. September 1, 2013.

Sec. 508.1445. ANNUAL REPORT ON GUIDELINES REQUIRED. (a) The board annually shall submit a report to the Criminal Justice Legislative Oversight Committee, the lieutenant governor, the speaker of the house of representatives, and the presiding officers of the standing committees in the senate and house of representatives primarily responsible for criminal justice regarding the board's application of the parole guidelines adopted under Section 508.144.

(b) The report must include:

(1) a brief explanation of the parole guidelines, including how the board:

(A) defines the risk factors and offense severity levels; and

(B) determines the range of recommended parole approval rates for each guideline score;

(2) a comparison of the range of recommended parole approval rates under the parole guidelines to the actual approval rates for individual parole panel members, regional offices, and the state as a whole; and

(3) a description of instances in which the actual parole approval rates do not meet the range of recommended parole approval rates under the parole guidelines, an explanation of the variations, and a list of actions

that the board has taken or will take to meet the guidelines.

Added by Acts 2007, 80th Leg., R.S., Ch. 1308 (S.B. 909), Sec. 40, eff. June 15, 2007.
Amended by:
Acts 2013, 83rd Leg., R.S., Ch. 1154 (S.B. 213), Sec. 16, eff. September 1, 2013.

Sec. 508.145. ELIGIBILITY FOR RELEASE ON PAROLE; COMPUTATION OF PAROLE ELIGIBILITY DATE. (a) An inmate is not eligible for release on parole if the inmate is under sentence of death, serving a sentence of life imprisonment without parole, or serving a sentence for any of the following offenses under the Penal Code:

(1) Section 20A.03, if the offense is based partly or wholly on conduct constituting an offense under Section 20A.02(a)(5), (6), (7), or (8);

(2) Section 21.02;

(3) Section 22.021, if the offense is punishable under Subsection (f) of that section; or

(4) Section 51.03 or 51.04.

(b) An inmate serving a life sentence under Section 12.31(a)(1), Penal Code, for a capital felony is not eligible for release on parole until the actual calendar time the inmate has served, without consideration of good conduct time, equals 40 calendar years.

(c) An inmate serving a sentence under Section 12.42(c)(2), Penal Code, is not eligible for release on parole until the actual calendar time the inmate has served, without consideration of good conduct time, equals 35 calendar years.

(c-1)(1) Except as provided by Subdivision (2), an inmate serving a sentence for an offense under Section 20A.02(a)(5), (6), (7), or (8), Penal Code, is not eligible for release on parole.

(2) An inmate serving a sentence for an offense described by Subdivision (1) for which the judgment in the case contains an affirmative finding under Article 42.01991, Code of Criminal Procedure, is not eligible for release on parole until the inmate's actual calendar time served, without consideration of good conduct time, equals one-half of the sentence or 30 calendar years, whichever is less, but in no event is the inmate eligible for release on parole in less than two calendar years.

(d)(1) This subsection applies only to an inmate who is serving a sentence for:

(A) an offense described by Article 42A.054(a), Code of Criminal Procedure, other than an offense under Section 19.03, Penal Code, or an offense under Chapter 20A, Penal Code, that is described by Subsection (a) (1) or (c-1)(1);

(B) an offense for which the judgment contains an affirmative finding under Article 42A.054(c) or (d), Code of Criminal Procedure; or

(C) an offense under Section 71.02 or 71.023, Penal Code.

(2) An inmate described by Subdivision (1) is not eligible for release on parole until the inmate's actual calendar time served, without consideration of good conduct time, equals one-half of the sentence or 30 calendar years, whichever is less, but in no event is the inmate eligible for release on parole in less than two calendar years.

(3) Notwithstanding Subdivision (2), an inmate who is serving a sentence for an offense under Section 22.021, Penal Code, is not eligible for release on parole if the inmate is serving a sentence for an offense for which punishment was enhanced under Section 12.42(c)(4), Penal Code.

(d-1) Notwithstanding Subsection (d), for every 12 months that elapse between the date an arrest warrant is issued for the inmate following an indictment for the offense and the date the inmate is arrested for the offense, the earliest date on which an inmate is eligible for parole is delayed by three years from the date otherwise provided by Subsection (d), if the inmate is serving a sentence for an offense under Section 19.02, 22.011, or 22.021, Penal Code.

(e) An inmate serving a sentence for which the punishment is increased under Section 481.134, Health and Safety Code, is not eligible for release on parole until the inmate's actual calendar time served, without consideration of good conduct time, equals five years or the term to which the inmate was sentenced, whichever is less.

(f) Except as provided by Section 508.146, any other inmate is eligible for release on parole when the inmate's actual calendar time served plus good conduct time equals one-fourth of the sentence imposed or 15 years, whichever is less.

Added by Acts 1997, 75th Leg., ch. 165, Sec. 12.01, eff. Sept. 1, 1997.
Amended by Acts 1999, 76th Leg., ch. 62, Sec. 10.21, eff. Sept. 1, 1999.
Amended by:

Acts 2005, 79th Leg., Ch. 787 (S.B. 60), Sec. 4, eff. September 1, 2005.

Acts 2005, 79th Leg., Ch. 787 (S.B. 60), Sec. 12, eff. September 1, 2005.

Acts 2007, 80th Leg., R.S., Ch. 405 (S.B. 877), Sec. 2, eff. September 1, 2007.

Acts 2007, 80th Leg., R.S., Ch. 593 (H.B. 8), Sec. 1.10, eff. September 1, 2007.

Acts 2009, 81st Leg., R.S., Ch. 146 (S.B. 1832), Sec. 2, eff. September

1, 2009.

Acts 2009, 81st Leg., R.S., Ch. 765 (S.B. 839), Sec. 2, eff. September 1, 2009.

Acts 2009, 81st Leg., R.S., Ch. 1400 (H.B. 221), Sec. 3, eff. September 1, 2009.

Acts 2011, 82nd Leg., R.S., Ch. 122 (H.B. 3000), Sec. 10, eff. September 1, 2011.

Acts 2011, 82nd Leg., R.S., Ch. 1119 (H.B. 3), Sec. 2, eff. September 1, 2011.

Acts 2013, 83rd Leg., R.S., Ch. 126 (S.B. 727), Sec. 2, eff. September 1, 2013.

Acts 2013, 83rd Leg., R.S., Ch. 1252 (H.B. 8), Sec. 13, eff. September 1, 2013.

Acts 2013, 83rd Leg., R.S., Ch. 1325 (S.B. 549), Sec. 2, eff. September 1, 2013.

Acts 2015, 84th Leg., R.S., Ch. 770 (H.B. 2299), Sec. 2.51, eff. January 1, 2017.

Acts 2021, 87th Leg., R.S., Ch. 632 (H.B. 465), Sec. 2, eff. September 1, 2021.

Acts 2021, 87th Leg., R.S., Ch. 632 (H.B. 465), Sec. 3, eff. September 1, 2021.

Acts 2023, 88th Leg., 4th C.S., Ch. 1 (S.B. 4), Sec. 6, eff. March 5, 2024.

Sec. 508.1455. EARLY RELEASE ON PAROLE FOR CERTAIN INMATES REQUIRED TO PARTICIPATE IN EDUCATIONAL AND VOCATIONAL TRAINING PILOT PROGRAM. (a) This section applies only to an inmate:

(1) who is serving a sentence for an offense under Chapter 481, Health and Safety Code, that is punishable as a felony of the third degree;

(2) who has not previously been convicted of a felony under Title 5, Penal Code, or under Chapter 43 or 71 of that code; and

(3) whose eligibility for parole is computed under Section 508.145(f).

(b) Notwithstanding any other law, a parole panel may release on parole an inmate described by Subsection (a) approximately 180 days before the date the inmate would be eligible for release on parole under Section 508.145(f).

(c) A parole panel releasing an inmate on parole under this section shall require as a condition of release on parole that the inmate participate in a program operated under Section 493.034, to begin immediately following the inmate's release on parole.

(d) For purpose of consideration by a parole panel for early release on parole under Subsection (b), the department shall annually identify not fewer than 100 inmates described by Subsection (a) who are suitable candidates for participation in a program operated under Section 493.034. The board and the department shall jointly adopt rules for identifying inmates under this subsection. The rules must require the board or the department to notify an inmate that the inmate is being considered for release on parole under this section.

(e) The board shall adopt rules governing the release of an inmate on parole under this section.

(f) An inmate who is considered for but not granted release on parole under this section shall be considered for release on parole on the date that the inmate otherwise would have been considered for release on parole under this chapter.

Added by Acts 2021, 87th Leg., R.S., Ch. 1014 (H.B. 2352), Sec. 4, eff. September 1, 2021.

Sec. 508.146. MEDICALLY RECOMMENDED INTENSIVE SUPERVISION. (a) An inmate other than an inmate who is serving a sentence of death or life without parole may be released on medically recommended intensive supervision on a date designated by a parole panel described by Subsection (e), except that an inmate with an instant offense that is an offense described in Article 42A.054, Code of Criminal Procedure, or an inmate who has a reportable conviction or adjudication under Chapter 62, Code of Criminal Procedure, may only be considered if a medical condition of terminal illness or long-term care has been diagnosed by a physician, if:

(1) the Texas Correctional Office on Offenders with Medical or Mental Impairments, in cooperation with the Correctional Managed Health Care Committee, identifies the inmate as being:

(A) a person who is elderly or terminally ill, a person with mental illness, an intellectual disability, or a physical disability, or a person who has a condition requiring long-term care, if the inmate is an inmate with an instant offense that is described in Article 42A.054, Code of Criminal Procedure; or

(B) in a persistent vegetative state or being a person with an organic brain syndrome with significant to total mobility impairment, if the inmate is an inmate who has a reportable conviction or adjudication under Chapter 62, Code of Criminal Procedure;

(2) the parole panel determines that, based on the inmate's condition and a medical evaluation, the inmate does not constitute a threat to public safety; and

(3) the Texas Correctional Office on Offenders with Medical or Mental Impairments, in cooperation with the pardons and paroles division, has prepared for the inmate a medically recommended intensive supervision plan that requires the inmate to submit to electronic monitoring, places the inmate on super-intensive supervision, or otherwise ensures appropriate supervision of the inmate.

(b) An inmate may be released on medically recommended intensive supervision only if the inmate's medically recommended intensive supervision plan under Subsection (a)(3) is approved by the Texas Correctional Office on Offenders with Medical or Mental Impairments.

(c) The parole panel shall require as a condition of release under Subsection (a) that the releasee remain under the care of a physician and in a medically suitable placement. At least once each calendar quarter, the Texas Correctional Office on Offenders with Medical or Mental Impairments shall report to the parole panel on the releasee's medical and placement status. On the basis of the report, the parole panel may modify conditions of release and impose any condition on the releasee that a panel could impose on a releasee released under Section 508.145, including a condition that the releasee reside in a halfway house or community residential facility.

(d) The Texas Correctional Office on Offenders with Medical or Mental Impairments and the Texas Department of Human Services shall jointly request proposals from public or private vendors to provide under contract services for inmates released on medically recommended intensive supervision. A request for proposals under this subsection may require that the services be provided in a medical care facility located in an urban area. For the purposes of this subsection, "urban area" means the area in this state within a metropolitan statistical area, according to the standards of the United States Bureau of the Census.

(e) Only parole panels composed of the presiding officer of the board and two members appointed to the panel by the presiding officer may make determinations regarding the release of inmates on medically recommended intensive supervision under Subsection (a) or of inmates released pending deportation. If the Texas Council on Offenders with Mental Impairments identifies an inmate as a candidate for release under the guidelines established by Subsection (a)(1), the council shall present to a parole panel described by this subsection relevant information concerning the inmate and the inmate's potential for release under this section.

(f) An inmate who is not a citizen of the United States, as defined by federal law, who is not under a sentence of death or life without parole, and who does not have a reportable conviction or adjudication under Chapter 62, Code of Criminal Procedure, or an instant offense described in Article

42A.054, Code of Criminal Procedure, may be released to immigration authorities pending deportation on a date designated by a parole panel described by Subsection (e) if the parole panel determines that on release the inmate would be deported to another country and that the inmate does not constitute a threat to public safety in the other country or this country and is unlikely to reenter this country illegally.

Added by Acts 1997, 75th Leg., ch. 165, Sec. 12.01, eff. Sept. 1, 1997.
Amended by Acts 2001, 77th Leg., ch. 1435, Sec. 1, eff. Sept. 1, 2001; Acts 2003, 78th Leg., ch. 252, Sec. 1, eff. Sept. 1, 2003; Acts 2003, 78th Leg., ch. 856, Sec. 21, eff. Sept. 1, 2003.
Amended by:

Acts 2005, 79th Leg., Ch. 787 (S.B. 60), Sec. 5, eff. September 1, 2005.

Acts 2007, 80th Leg., R.S., Ch. 1247 (H.B. 2611), Sec. 1, eff. September 1, 2007.

Acts 2015, 84th Leg., R.S., Ch. 770 (H.B. 2299), Sec. 2.52, eff. January 1, 2017.

Sec. 508.147. RELEASE TO MANDATORY SUPERVISION. (a) Except as provided by Section 508.149, a parole panel shall order the release of an inmate who is not on parole to mandatory supervision when the actual calendar time the inmate has served plus any accrued good conduct time equals the term to which the inmate was sentenced.

(b) An inmate released to mandatory supervision is considered to be released on parole.

(c) To the extent practicable, arrangements for the inmate's proper employment, maintenance, and care must be made before the inmate's release to mandatory supervision.

Added by Acts 1997, 75th Leg., ch. 165, Sec. 12.01, eff. Sept. 1, 1997.

Sec. 508.1471. RELEASE TO MANDATORY SUPERVISION OF CERTAIN INMATES CONFINED IN COUNTY JAIL. (a) This section applies only to an inmate who, at the time the inmate is sentenced to a term of imprisonment in the department, is:

(1) confined in a county jail; and

(2) eligible for immediate release to mandatory supervision.

(b) Before an inmate is released from a county jail to mandatory supervision, the department shall provide notice to a victim, guardian of a victim, or close relative of a deceased victim that the inmate is eligible for release to mandatory supervision. The notice must be sent to the address provided in the victim impact statement or submitted under Section 508.117(b) and must state that the victim, guardian, or close relative may submit, not later than the 14th day after the date of the notice, a written statement to the parole panel considering the inmate's release regarding:

(1) the offense;

(2) the inmate; and

(3) the effect of the offense on the victim, guardian, or close relative.

(c) Notwithstanding any other law, the parole panel may interview a victim, guardian of a victim, or close relative of a deceased victim regarding the release of the inmate to mandatory supervision.

(d) In this section, "victim," "guardian of a victim," and "close relative of a deceased victim" have the meanings assigned by Section 508.117.

Added by Acts 2021, 87th Leg., R.S., Ch. 636 (H.B. 721), Sec. 1, eff. September 1, 2021.

Sec. 508.148. PERIOD OF MANDATORY SUPERVISION. (a) The period of mandatory supervision is computed by subtracting from the term for which the inmate was sentenced the calendar time served on the sentence.

(b) The time served on mandatory supervision is computed as calendar time.

Added by Acts 1997, 75th Leg., ch. 165, Sec. 12.01, eff. Sept. 1, 1997.

Sec. 508.149. INMATES INELIGIBLE FOR MANDATORY SUPERVISION. (a) An inmate may not be released to mandatory supervision if the inmate is serving a sentence for or has been previously convicted of:

(1) an offense for which the judgment contains an affirmative finding under Article 42A.054(c) or (d), Code of Criminal Procedure;

(2) a first degree felony or a second degree felony under Section 19.02, Penal Code;

(3) a capital felony under Section 19.03, Penal Code;

(4) a first degree felony or a second degree felony under Section 20.04, Penal Code;

(5) an offense under Section 21.11, Penal Code;

(6) a felony under Section 22.011, Penal Code;

(7) a first degree felony or a second degree felony under Section 22.02, Penal Code;

(8) a first degree felony under Section 22.021, Penal Code;

(9) a first degree felony under Section 22.04, Penal Code;

(10) a first degree felony under Section 28.02, Penal Code;

(11) a second degree felony under Section 29.02, Penal Code;

(12) a first degree felony under Section 29.03, Penal Code;

(13) a first degree felony under Section 30.02, Penal Code;

(14) a felony for which the punishment is increased under Section 481.134 or 481.140, Health and Safety Code;

(15) an offense under Section 43.25, Penal Code;

(16) an offense under Section 21.02, Penal Code;

(17) a first degree felony under Section 15.03, Penal Code;

(18) an offense under Section 43.05, Penal Code;

(19) an offense under Section 20A.02, Penal Code;

(20) an offense under Section 20A.03, Penal Code;

(21) a first degree felony under Section 71.02 or 71.023, Penal Code;

(22) an offense under Section 481.1123, Health and Safety Code, punished under Subsection (d), (e), or (f) of that section;

(23) a second degree felony under Section 22.01, Penal Code; or

(24) an offense under Section 22.01, Penal Code, punished under Subsection (b)(2), (7), or (8) of that section.

(a-1) An inmate serving a sentence for an offense under Section 51.03 or 51.04, Penal Code, may not be released to mandatory supervision.

(b) An inmate may not be released to mandatory supervision if a parole panel determines that:

(1) the inmate's accrued good conduct time is not an accurate reflection of the inmate's potential for rehabilitation; and

(2) the inmate's release would endanger the public.

(c) A parole panel that makes a determination under Subsection (b) shall specify in writing the reasons for the determination.

(d) A determination under Subsection (b) is not subject to administrative or judicial review, except that the parole panel making the determination shall reconsider the inmate for release to mandatory supervision at least twice during the two years after the date of the determination.

Added by Acts 1997, 75th Leg., ch. 165, Sec. 12.01, eff. Sept. 1, 1997.
Amended by Acts 1999, 76th Leg., ch. 62, Sec. 10.22, eff. Sept. 1, 1999; Acts 2001, 77th Leg., ch. 786, Sec. 3, eff. June 14, 2001.
Amended by:

Acts 2007, 80th Leg., R.S., Ch. 593 (H.B. 8), Sec. 1.11, eff. September 1, 2007.

Acts 2009, 81st Leg., R.S., Ch. 146 (S.B. 1832), Sec. 3, eff. September 1, 2009.

Acts 2011, 82nd Leg., R.S., Ch. 1 (S.B. 24), Sec. 5.02, eff. September 1, 2011.

Acts 2011, 82nd Leg., R.S., Ch. 122 (H.B. 3000), Sec. 11, eff. September 1, 2011.

Acts 2013, 83rd Leg., R.S., Ch. 161 (S.B. 1093), Sec. 9.011, eff. September 1, 2013.

Acts 2013, 83rd Leg., R.S., Ch. 1325 (S.B. 549), Sec. 3, eff. September 1, 2013.

Acts 2015, 84th Leg., R.S., Ch. 770 (H.B. 2299), Sec. 2.53, eff. January 1, 2017.

Acts 2021, 87th Leg., R.S., Ch. 584 (S.B. 768), Sec. 16, eff. September 1, 2021.

Acts 2023, 88th Leg., R.S., Ch. 692 (H.B. 1577), Sec. 1, eff. September 1, 2023.

Acts 2023, 88th Leg., 4th C.S., Ch. 1 (S.B. 4), Sec. 7, eff. March 5, 2024.

Sec. 508.150. CONSECUTIVE FELONY SENTENCES. (a) If an inmate is sentenced to consecutive felony sentences under Article 42.08, Code of Criminal Procedure, a parole panel shall designate during each sentence the date, if any, the inmate would have been eligible for release on parole if the inmate had been sentenced to serve a single sentence.

(b) For the purposes of Article 42.08, Code of Criminal Procedure, the judgment and sentence of an inmate sentenced for a felony, other than the last sentence in a series of consecutive sentences, cease to operate:

(1) when the actual calendar time served by the inmate equals the sentence imposed by the court; or

(2) on the date a parole panel designates as the date the inmate would have been eligible for release on parole if the inmate had been sentenced to serve a single sentence.

(c) A parole panel may not:

(1) consider consecutive sentences as a single sentence for purposes of parole; or

(2) release on parole an inmate sentenced to serve consecutive felony sentences before the date the inmate becomes eligible for release on parole from the last sentence imposed on the inmate.

(d) A parole panel may not use calendar time served and good conduct time accrued by an inmate that are used by the panel in determining when a judgment and sentence cease to operate:

(1) for the same purpose in determining that date in a subsequent sentence in the same series of consecutive sentences; or

(2) for determining the date an inmate becomes eligible for release on parole from the last sentence in a series of consecutive sentences.

Added by Acts 1997, 75th Leg., ch. 165, Sec. 12.01, eff. Sept. 1, 1997.

Sec. 508.151. PRESUMPTIVE PAROLE DATE. (a) For the purpose of diverting inmates to halfway houses under Section 508.118, a parole panel, after reviewing all available pertinent information, may designate a presumptive parole date for an inmate who:

(1) has never been convicted of an offense listed under Article 42A.054(a), Code of Criminal Procedure, or an offense under Section 21.02, Penal Code; and

(2) has never had a conviction with a judgment that contains an affirmative finding under Article 42A.054(c) or (d), Code of Criminal Procedure.

(b) The presumptive parole date may not be a date that is earlier than the inmate's initial parole eligibility date computed under Section 508.145.

(c) A parole panel may rescind or postpone a previously established presumptive parole date on the basis of a report from an agent of the division responsible for supervision or an agent of the institutional division acting in the case.

(d) If an inmate transferred to preparole status has satisfactorily served the inmate's sentence in the halfway house to which the inmate is assigned from the date of transfer to the presumptive parole date, without rescission or postponement of the date, the parole panel shall order the inmate's release on parole and issue an appropriate certificate of release. The releasee is subject to the provisions of this chapter governing release on parole.

Added by Acts 1997, 75th Leg., ch. 165, Sec. 12.01, eff. Sept. 1, 1997.
Amended by:

Acts 2007, 80th Leg., R.S., Ch. 593 (H.B. 8), Sec. 3.40, eff. September 1, 2007.

Acts 2011, 82nd Leg., R.S., Ch. 122 (H.B. 3000), Sec. 12, eff. September 1, 2011.

Acts 2015, 84th Leg., R.S., Ch. 770 (H.B. 2299), Sec. 2.54, eff. January 1, 2017.

Acts 2023, 88th Leg., R.S., Ch. 768 (H.B. 4595), Sec. 10.007, eff. September 1, 2023.

Sec. 508.152. INDIVIDUAL TREATMENT PLAN. (a) Not later than the 120th day after the date an inmate is admitted to the institutional division, the department shall obtain all pertinent information relating to the inmate, including:

(1) the court judgment;

(2) any sentencing report;

(3) the circumstances of the inmate's offense;

(4) the inmate's previous social history and criminal record;

(5) the inmate's physical and mental health record;

(6) a record of the inmate's conduct, employment history, and attitude in the institutional division; and

(7) any written comments or information provided by local trial officials or victims of the offense.

(b) The department shall:

(1) establish for the inmate an individual treatment plan; and

(2) submit the plan to the board at the time of the board's consideration of the inmate's case for release.

(b-1) The department shall include in an inmate's individual treatment plan:

(1) a record of the inmate's institutional progress that includes the inmate's participation in any program, including an intensive volunteer program as defined by the department;

(2) the results of any assessment of the inmate, including any assessment made using the risk and needs assessment instrument adopted under Section 501.0921 and any vocational, educational, or substance abuse assessment;

(3) the dates on which the inmate must participate in any subsequent assessment; and

(4) all of the treatment and programming needs of the inmate, prioritized based on the inmate's assessed needs.

(b-2) At least once in every 12-month period, the department shall review each inmate's individual treatment plan to assess the inmate's institutional progress and revise or update the plan as necessary. The department shall make reasonable efforts to provide an inmate the opportunity to complete any classes or programs included in the inmate's individual treatment plan, other than classes or programs that are to be completed immediately before the inmate's release on parole, in a timely manner so that the inmate's release on parole is not delayed due to any uncompleted classes or programs.

(c) The board shall conduct an initial review of an eligible inmate not later than the 180th day after the date of the inmate's admission to the institutional division. The board shall identify any classes or programs that the board intends to require the inmate to complete before releasing the inmate on parole. The department shall provide the inmate with a list of those classes or programs.

(d) Before the inmate is approved for release on parole, the inmate must agree to participate in the programs and activities described by the individual treatment plan.

(e) The institutional division shall:

(1) work closely with the board to monitor the progress of the inmate in the institutional division; and

(2) report the progress to the board before the inmate's release.

(f) An attorney representing the state in the prosecution of an inmate serving a sentence for an offense described by Section 508.187(a) shall provide written comments to the department on the circumstances related to the commission of the offense and other information determined by the attorney to be relevant to any subsequent parole decisions regarding the inmate.

Added by Acts 1997, 75th Leg., ch. 165, Sec. 12.01, eff. Sept. 1, 1997.
Amended by Acts 2001, 77th Leg., ch. 978, Sec. 1, eff. Sept. 1, 2001.
Amended by:

Acts 2013, 83rd Leg., R.S., Ch. 1154 (S.B. 213), Sec. 17, eff. September 1, 2013.

Acts 2013, 83rd Leg., R.S., Ch. 1154 (S.B. 213), Sec. 18, eff. September 1, 2013.

Acts 2017, 85th Leg., R.S., Ch. 505 (H.B. 2888), Sec. 1, eff. September 1, 2017.

Sec. 508.153. STATEMENTS OF VICTIM. (a) A parole panel considering for release on parole or mandatory supervision an inmate who is serving a sentence for an offense in which a person was a victim shall allow:

(1) the victim, a guardian of the victim, a close relative of the deceased victim, or a representative of the victim, the victim's guardian, or the victim's close relative to provide a written statement to the panel; and

(2) the victim, guardian of the victim, or close relative of the deceased victim to appear in person before the board members to present a statement of the person's views about:

(A) the offense;

(B) the inmate; and

(C) the effect of the offense on the victim.

(b) If more than one person is entitled to appear in person before the board members or parole commissioners, only the person chosen by all persons entitled to appear as the persons' sole representative may appear.

(c) The panel shall consider the statements and the information provided in a victim impact statement in determining whether to recommend an inmate for release on parole.

(d) This section does not limit the number of persons who may provide written statements for or against the release of the inmate on parole.

(e) In this section:

(1) "Close relative of a deceased victim" means a person who, regardless of whether the victim's death was related to the offense committed, was:

(A) the spouse of the victim at the time of the victim's death;

(B) a parent of the deceased victim;

(C) an adult brother, sister, or child of the deceased victim; or

(D) the nearest relative of the deceased victim by consanguinity, if the persons described by Paragraphs (A) through (C) are deceased or are incapacitated due to physical or mental illness or infirmity.

(2) "Guardian of a victim" and "victim" have the meanings assigned by Section 508.117.

Added by Acts 1997, 75th Leg., ch. 165, Sec. 12.01, eff. Sept. 1, 1997. Amended by Acts 2001, 77th Leg., ch. 856, Sec. 6, eff. Sept. 1, 2001; Acts 2003, 78th Leg., 3rd C.S., ch. 3, Sec. 11.19, eff. Jan. 11, 2004.
Amended by:

Acts 2023, 88th Leg., R.S., Ch. 471 (H.B. 517), Sec. 2, eff. September 1, 2023.

Sec. 508.1531. CONTACT WITH VICTIM. A parole panel considering the release of an inmate on parole or to mandatory supervision may consider whether the inmate violated a policy adopted by the department under Section 498.0042(a) or a court order entered under Article 42.24, Code of Criminal Procedure.

Added by Acts 2011, 82nd Leg., R.S., Ch. 491 (H.B. 1028), Sec. 4, eff. September 1, 2011.

Sec. 508.154. CONTRACT ON RELEASE. (a) An inmate to be released on parole shall be furnished a contract stating in clear and intelligible language the conditions and rules of parole.

(b) Acceptance, signing, and execution of the contract by the inmate to be paroled is a precondition to release on parole.

(c) An inmate released to mandatory supervision shall be furnished a written statement stating in clear and intelligible language the conditions and rules of mandatory supervision.

(d) A releasee while on parole or mandatory supervision must be amenable to the conditions of supervision ordered by a parole panel.

Added by Acts 1997, 75th Leg., ch. 165, Sec. 12.01, eff. Sept. 1, 1997.

Sec. 508.155. COMPLETION OF PAROLE PERIOD. (a) To complete a parole period, a releasee must serve the entire period of parole.

(b) The time on parole is computed as calendar time.

(c) The division may allow a releasee to serve the remainder of the releasee's sentence without supervision and without being required to report if a parole supervisor at the regional level has approved the releasee's early release from supervision under Section 508.1555.

(d) The division may require a person released from supervision and reporting under Subsection (c) to resubmit to supervision and resume reporting at any time and for any reason.

Added by Acts 1997, 75th Leg., ch. 165, Sec. 12.01, eff. Sept. 1, 1997.
Amended by:

Acts 2007, 80th Leg., R.S., Ch. 1308 (S.B. 909), Sec. 41, eff. June 15, 2007.

Sec. 508.1555. PROCEDURE FOR THE EARLY RELEASE FROM SUPERVISION OF CERTAIN RELEASEES. (a) A parole officer annually shall identify the releasees under the parole officer's supervision who are eligible for early release from supervision under Section 508.155(c). A releasee is eligible for early release if:

(1) the releasee has been under supervision for at least one-half of the time that remained on the releasee's sentence when the releasee was released from imprisonment;

(2) during the preceding two-year period, the releasee has not committed any violation of the rules or conditions of release;

(3) during the period of supervision the releasee's parole or release to mandatory supervision has not been revoked; and

(4) the division determines:

(A) that the releasee has made a good faith effort to comply with any restitution order imposed on the releasee by a court; and

(B) that allowing the releasee to serve the remainder of the releasee's sentence without supervision and reporting is in the best interest of society.

(b) After identifying any releasees who are eligible for early release under Subsection (a), the parole officer shall review the eligible releasees, including any releasees the parole officer has previously declined to recommend for early release, to determine if a recommendation for early release from supervision is appropriate. In conducting the review and determining recommendations, the parole officer shall consider whether the releasee:

(1) has a low risk of recidivism as determined by an assessment developed by the department; and

(2) has made a good faith effort to comply with the conditions of release.

(c) A parole officer shall forward to the parole supervisor at the regional level any recommendations for early release the parole officer makes under Subsection (b). If the parole supervisor approves the recommendation, the division shall allow a releasee to serve the remainder of the releasee's sentence without supervision and without being required to report as authorized by Section 508.155.

Added by Acts 2007, 80th Leg., R.S., Ch. 1308 (S.B. 909), Sec. 42, eff. June 15, 2007.

Sec. 508.156. DETERMINATE SENTENCE PAROLE. (a) Before the release of a person who is transferred under Section 152.0016(g), 152.00161(e), 245.051(c), or 245.151(e), Human Resources Code, to the department for release on parole, a parole panel shall review the person's records and may interview the person or any other person the panel considers necessary to determine the conditions of parole. The panel may impose any reasonable condition of parole on the person that the panel may impose on an adult inmate under this chapter.

(b) The panel shall furnish the person with a written statement clearly describing the conditions and rules of parole. The person must accept and sign the statement as a precondition to release on parole.

(c) While on parole, the person remains in the legal custody of the state and shall comply with the conditions of parole ordered by a panel under this section.

(d) The period of parole for a person released on parole under this section is the term for which the person was sentenced less calendar time served at the Texas Juvenile Justice Department or in the custody of a juvenile board or local juvenile probation department following a commitment under Section 54.04011(c)(2), Family Code, and in a juvenile detention facility in connection with the conduct for which the person was adjudicated.

(e) If a parole panel revokes the person's parole, the panel may require the person to serve the remaining portion of the person's sentence in the institutional division. The remaining portion of the person's sentence is computed without credit for the time from the date of the person's release to the date of revocation. The panel may not recommit the person to the Texas Juvenile Justice Department or to the custody of a juvenile board or local juvenile probation department.

(f) For purposes of this chapter, a person released from the Texas Juvenile Justice Department or the custody of a juvenile board or local juvenile probation department on parole under this section is considered to have been convicted of the offense for which the person has been adjudicated.

Added by Acts 1997, 75th Leg., ch. 165, Sec. 12.01, eff. Sept. 1, 1997.
Amended by:

Acts 2007, 80th Leg., R.S., Ch. 263 (S.B. 103), Sec. 19, eff. June 8, 2007.

Acts 2011, 82nd Leg., R.S., Ch. 85 (S.B. 653), Sec. 3.014, eff. September 1, 2011.

Acts 2015, 84th Leg., R.S., Ch. 734 (H.B. 1549), Sec. 101, eff. September 1, 2015.

Acts 2015, 84th Leg., R.S., Ch. 854 (S.B. 1149), Sec. 7, eff. September 1, 2015.

Sec. 508.157. TEMPORARY HOUSING ON RELEASE. (a) This section applies only to inmates who are eligible for release on parole or to mandatory supervision and to releasees.

(a-1) In this section, "residential correctional facility" means a facility operated by or under contract with the department to provide housing, supervision, and programmatic support to individuals released on parole or to mandatory supervision. The term includes a halfway house described by Section 508.118 or a community residential facility described by Section 508.119. The term does not include a transitional treatment center, a substance abuse felony punishment facility, or any other facility operated by or under contract with the department the primary purpose of which is to provide substance abuse treatment or aftercare.

(b) If the department does not operate or contract for the operation of a residential correctional facility in the county of legal residence of an inmate or releasee, the department may issue, for an inmate described by Subsection (a) or for a releasee, payment for the cost of temporary post-release housing that:

(1) meets any conditions or requirements imposed by a parole panel;

(2) is located in the county of legal residence of the inmate or

releasee; and

(3) except as provided by Subsection (e-1), is in a structure that existed on June 1, 2009, as a multifamily residence or as a motel to which Section 156.001, Tax Code, applies.

(c) The amount of payment issued under Subsection (b) may not exceed an amount that is equal to the cost the department would incur, for the period for which the payment is issued, to:

(1) incarcerate the inmate or releasee in a facility operated by or under contract with the department; or

(2) house the inmate or releasee in a residential correctional facility.

(d) The department shall issue payment under Subsection (b) out of funds appropriated by the legislature to the department for use in administering the parole system with respect to the housing of inmates on their release.

(e) The executive director of the Texas Department of Criminal Justice shall adopt rules as necessary to implement this section.

(e-1) The department may issue payment for post-release housing under Subsection (b) for a structure not described by Subsection (b)(3) if, before issuing payment, the department or the owner of the structure provides, in the same manner as required for a community corrections facility under Section 509.010, notice of the proposed use of the structure under this section and a hearing on the issue of whether the use is appropriate.

Added by Acts 2009, 81st Leg., R.S., Ch. 944 (H.B. 3226), Sec. 1, eff. June 19, 2009.

Amended by:

Acts 2011, 82nd Leg., R.S., Ch. 286 (H.B. 1770), Sec. 1, eff. June 17, 2011.

SUBCHAPTER E-1. ALTERNATIVE HOUSING IN CERTAIN COUNTIES

Sec. 508.171. APPLICABILITY. This subchapter applies only with respect to alternative housing that is located in a county with a population of 3.3 million or more.

Added by Acts 2021, 87th Leg., R.S., Ch. 462 (H.B. 954), Sec. 2, eff. September 1, 2021.

Sec. 508.172. ALTERNATIVE HOUSING PROGRAM. The department shall require that an applicant to participate as a provider in a program designed to provide alternative housing for two or more unrelated releasees submit with the application, in the manner specified by the department, a permit or other documentation showing that the proposed alternative housing facility is in compliance with all applicable municipal and county regulations.

Added by Acts 2021, 87th Leg., R.S., Ch. 462 (H.B. 954), Sec. 2, eff. September 1, 2021.

Sec. 508.173. INFORMATION REGARDING ALTERNATIVE HOUSING; NOTICE TO POLITICAL SUBDIVISION. (a) The department shall maintain the following information regarding releasees:

(1) a list of facilities providing alternative housing to two or more unrelated releasees, including:

(A) the name, address, and telephone number of the facility;

(B) the county in which the facility is located;

(C) information regarding whether the facility is in compliance with all applicable municipal and county regulations;

(D) the number of releasees residing at the facility; and

(E) the maximum capacity of the facility; and

(2) a list of releasees being housed at a facility described by Subdivision (1), including:

(A) the releasee's name;

(B) the county in which the releasee is required to reside under Section 508.181;

(C) the county in which the releasee committed the offense for which the releasee is on parole or mandatory supervision;

(D) the alternative housing facility in which the releasee resides; and

(E) the date on which the releasee began residing at the facility.

(b) On request of a county or municipality, the department shall provide monthly the information maintained by the department under Subsection (a). A county or municipality shall notify the department if the county or municipality does not want to continue to receive the information.

(c) The department shall provide the information to a county or municipality under Subsection (b) by secured electronic mail and in a machine-readable format.

(d) On request by a member of the legislature, the department shall provide the information maintained by the department under Subsection (a) to the member.

Added by Acts 2021, 87th Leg., R.S., Ch. 462 (H.B. 954), Sec. 2, eff.

September 1, 2021.

SUBCHAPTER F. MANDATORY CONDITIONS OF PAROLE OR MANDATORY SUPERVISION

Sec. 508.181. RESIDENCE DURING RELEASE. (a) Except as provided by Subsections (b) and (c), a parole panel shall require as a condition of parole or mandatory supervision that the releasee reside in the county in which:

(1) the releasee resided at the time of committing the offense for which the releasee was sentenced to the institutional division; or

(2) the releasee committed the offense for which the releasee was sentenced to the institutional division, if the releasee was not a resident of this state at the time of committing the offense.

(b) A parole panel may require a releasee to reside in a county other than the county required under Subsection (a) to:

(1) protect the life or safety of:

(A) a victim of the releasee's offense;

(B) the releasee;

(C) a witness in the case; or

(D) any other person; or

(2) increase the likelihood of the releasee's successful completion of parole or mandatory supervision, because of:

(A) written expressions of significant public concern in the county in which the releasee would otherwise be required to reside;

(B) the presence of family members or friends in the other county who have expressed a willingness to assist the releasee in successfully completing the conditions of the releasee's parole or mandatory supervision;

(C) the verified existence of a job offer in the other county; or

(D) the availability of a treatment program, educational program, or other social service program in the other county that is not available in the county in which the releasee is otherwise required to reside under Subsection (a).

(c) At any time after a releasee is released on parole or to mandatory supervision, a parole panel may modify the conditions of parole or mandatory supervision to require the releasee to reside in a county other than the county required by the original conditions. In making a decision under this subsection, a parole panel must consider the factors listed under Subsection (b).

(d) If a parole panel initially requires the releasee to reside in a county other than the county required under Subsection (a), the parole panel shall subsequently require the releasee to reside in the county described under Subsection (a) if the requirement that the releasee reside in the other county was based on:

(1) the verified existence of a job offer under Subsection (b)(2)(C) and the releasee is no longer employed or actively seeking employment; or

(2) the availability of a treatment program, educational program, or other social service program under Subsection (b)(2)(D) and the releasee:

(A) no longer regularly participates in the program as required by a condition of parole or mandatory supervision; or

(B) has successfully completed the program but has violated another condition of the releasee's parole or mandatory supervision.

(e) If a parole panel requires the releasee to reside in a county other than the county required under Subsection (a), the panel shall:

(1) state in writing the reason for the panel's decision; and

(2) place the statement in the releasee's permanent record.

(f) This section does not apply to a decision by a parole panel to require a releasee to serve the period of parole or mandatory supervision in another state.

(g) The division shall, on the first working day of each month, notify the sheriff of any county in which the total number of sex offenders under the supervision and control of the division residing in the county exceeds 10 percent of the total number of sex offenders in the state under the supervision and control of the division. The notice must be provided by e-mail or other electronic communication. If the total number of sex offenders under the supervision and control of the division residing in a county exceeds 22 percent of the total number of sex offenders in the state under the supervision and control of the division, a parole panel may require a sex offender to reside in that county only as required by Subsection (a) or for the reason stated in Subsection (b)(2)(B). In this subsection, "sex offender" means a person who is released on parole or to mandatory supervision after serving a sentence for an offense described by Section 508.187(a).

(h) If a parole panel requires a releasee to reside in a county other than the county required under Subsection (a), the division shall include the reason for residency exemption in the required notification to the sheriff of the county in which the defendant is to reside, the chief of police of the municipality in which the halfway house is located, and the attorney who represents the state in the prosecution of felonies in that county.

Added by Acts 1997, 75th Leg., ch. 165, Sec. 12.01, eff. Sept. 1, 1997.
Amended by Acts 1999, 76th Leg., ch. 62, Sec. 10.23, 10.24, eff. Sept. 1, 1999.
Amended by:

Acts 2011, 82nd Leg., R.S., Ch. 1123 (H.B. 200), Sec. 6, eff. September 1, 2011.

Sec. 508.182. PAROLE SUPERVISION FEE; ADMINISTRATIVE FEE. (a) A parole panel shall require as a condition of parole or mandatory supervision that a releasee pay to the division for each month during which the releasee is under parole supervision:

(1) a parole supervision fee of $10; and

(2) an administrative fee of $8.

(b) A fee under this section applies to an inmate released in another state who is required as a condition of the inmate's release to report to a parole officer or supervisor in this state for parole supervision.

(c) On the request of the releasee, a parole panel may allow the releasee to defer one or more payments under this section. The releasee remains responsible for payment of the fee and shall pay the amount of the deferred payment not later than the second anniversary of the date the payment becomes due.

(d) The Texas Board of Criminal Justice shall adopt rules relating to the method of payment required of the releasee.

(e) The division shall remit fees collected under this section to the comptroller. The comptroller shall deposit the fees collected under:

(1) Subsection (a)(1) in the general revenue fund; and

(2) Subsection (a)(2) in the compensation to victims of crime fund.

(f) In a parole or mandatory supervision revocation hearing under Section 508.281 at which it is alleged only that the releasee failed to make a payment under this section, it is an affirmative defense to revocation that the releasee is unable to pay the amount as ordered by a parole panel. The releasee must prove the affirmative defense by a preponderance of the evidence.

Added by Acts 1997, 75th Leg., ch. 165, Sec. 12.01, eff. Sept. 1, 1997.

Sec. 508.183. EDUCATIONAL SKILL LEVEL. (a) A parole panel shall require as a condition of release on parole or release to mandatory supervision that an inmate demonstrate to the parole panel whether the inmate has an educational skill level that is equal to or greater than the average skill level of students who have completed the sixth grade in a public school in this state.

(b) If the parole panel determines that the inmate has not attained that skill level, the parole panel shall require as a condition of parole or mandatory supervision that the inmate as a releasee attain that level of educational skill, unless the parole panel determines that the inmate lacks the intellectual capacity or the learning ability to ever achieve that level of skill.

Added by Acts 1997, 75th Leg., ch. 165, Sec. 12.01, eff. Sept. 1, 1997.

Sec. 508.184. CONTROLLED SUBSTANCE TESTING. (a) A parole panel shall require as a condition of parole or mandatory supervision that a releasee submit to testing for controlled substances on evidence that:

(1) a controlled substance is present in the releasee's body;

(2) the releasee has used a controlled substance; or

(3) the use of a controlled substance is related to the offense for which the releasee was convicted.

(b) The Texas Board of Criminal Justice by rule shall adopt procedures for the administration of a test required under this section.

Added by Acts 1997, 75th Leg., ch. 165, Sec. 12.01, eff. Sept. 1, 1997.

Sec. 508.185. SUBSTANCE ABUSE TREATMENT. (a) A parole panel shall require as a condition of release on parole or release to mandatory supervision that an inmate who immediately before release is a participant in the program established under Section 501.0931 participate as a releasee in a drug or alcohol abuse continuum of care treatment program.

(b) The Texas Commission on Alcohol and Drug Abuse shall develop the continuum of care treatment program.

Added by Acts 1997, 75th Leg., ch. 165, Sec. 12.01, eff. Sept. 1, 1997.

Sec. 508.186. SEX OFFENDER REGISTRATION. A parole panel shall require as a condition of parole or mandatory supervision that a releasee required to register as a sex offender under Chapter 62, Code of Criminal Procedure:

(1) register under that chapter; and

(2) submit a blood sample or other specimen to the Department of Public Safety under Subchapter G, Chapter 411, for the purpose of creating a DNA record of the releasee, unless the releasee has already submitted the required specimen under other state law.

Added by Acts 1997, 75th Leg., ch. 165, Sec. 12.01, eff. Sept. 1, 1997.
Amended by Acts 1999, 76th Leg., ch. 62, Sec. 10.25, eff. Sept. 1, 1999; Acts 2001, 77th Leg., ch. 211, Sec. 16, eff. Sept. 1, 2001; Acts 2003, 78th Leg., ch. 1300, Sec. 9, eff. Sept. 1, 2003.
Amended by:

Acts 2005, 79th Leg., Ch. 1008 (H.B. 867), Sec. 1.06, eff. September 1, 2005.

Sec. 508.1861. PROHIBITIONS ON INTERNET ACCESS FOR CERTAIN SEX OFFENDERS. (a) This section applies only to a person who, on release, will be required to register as a sex offender under Chapter 62, Code of Criminal Procedure, by court order or otherwise, and:

(1) is serving a sentence for an offense under Section 21.11, 22.011(a)(2), 22.021(a)(1)(B), 33.021, or 43.25, Penal Code;

(2) used the Internet or any other type of electronic device used for Internet access to commit the offense or engage in the conduct for which the person is required to register under Chapter 62, Code of Criminal Procedure; or

(3) is assigned a numeric risk level of two or three based on an assessment conducted under Article 62.007, Code of Criminal Procedure.

(b) If the parole panel releases on parole or to mandatory supervision a person described by Subsection (a), the parole panel as a condition of parole or mandatory supervision shall:

(1) prohibit the releasee from using the Internet to:

(A) access material that is obscene as defined by Section 43.21, Penal Code;

(B) access a commercial social networking site, as defined by Article 62.0061(f), Code of Criminal Procedure;

(C) communicate with any individual concerning sexual relations with an individual who is younger than 17 years of age; or

(D) communicate with another individual the releasee knows is younger than 17 years of age; and

(2) to ensure the releasee's compliance with Subdivision (1), require the releasee to submit to regular inspection or monitoring of each electronic device used by the releasee to access the Internet.

(c) The parole panel may modify at any time the condition described by Subsection (b)(1)(D) if:

(1) the condition interferes with the releasee's ability to attend school or become or remain employed and consequently constitutes an undue hardship for the releasee; or

(2) the releasee is the parent or guardian of an individual who is younger than 17 years of age and the releasee is not otherwise prohibited from communicating with that individual.

Added by Acts 2009, 81st Leg., R.S., Ch. 755 (S.B. 689), Sec. 10, eff. September 1, 2009.

Amended by:

Acts 2015, 84th Leg., R.S., Ch. 684 (H.B. 372), Sec. 2, eff. September 1, 2015.

Sec. 508.1862. SEX OFFENDER TREATMENT. A parole panel shall require as a condition of release on parole or to mandatory supervision that a releasee participate in a sex offender treatment program developed by the department if:

(1) the releasee:

(A) was serving a sentence for an offense under Chapter 21, Penal Code; or

(B) is required to register as a sex offender under Chapter 62, Code of Criminal Procedure; and

(2) immediately before release, the releasee is participating in a sex offender treatment program established under Section 499.054.

Added by Acts 2015, 84th Leg., R.S., Ch. 1114 (H.B. 3387), Sec. 1, eff. September 1, 2015.

Sec. 508.1864. NOTIFICATION TO DEPARTMENT OF PUBLIC SAFETY AND LICENSING AUTHORITY. (a) In this section, "health care professional," "license," and "licensing authority" have the meanings assigned by Section 108.051, Occupations Code.

(b) A parole panel that knows an inmate holds or has submitted an application for a license as a health care professional shall immediately notify the Department of Public Safety and the applicable licensing authority if the parole panel requires the inmate as a condition of release on parole or to mandatory supervision to register as a sex offender under Chapter 62, Code of Criminal Procedure.

Added by Acts 2019, 86th Leg., R.S., Ch. 789 (H.B. 1899), Sec. 4, eff. September 1, 2019.

Sec. 508.187. CHILD SAFETY ZONE. (a) This section applies only to a releasee serving a sentence for an offense under:

(1) Section 43.25 or 43.26, Penal Code;

(2) Section 21.02, 21.11, 22.011, 22.021, or 25.02, Penal Code;

(3) Section 20.04(a)(4), Penal Code, if the releasee committed the offense with the intent to violate or abuse the victim sexually;

(4) Section 30.02, Penal Code, punishable under Subsection (d) of that section, if the releasee committed the offense with the intent to commit

a felony listed in Subdivision (2) or (3);

(5) Section 43.05(a)(2), Penal Code; or

(6) Section 20A.02, Penal Code, if the defendant:

(A) trafficked the victim with the intent or knowledge that the victim would engage in sexual conduct, as defined by Section 43.25, Penal Code; or

(B) benefited from participating in a venture that involved a trafficked victim engaging in sexual conduct, as defined by Section 43.25, Penal Code.

(b) A parole panel shall establish a child safety zone applicable to a releasee if the panel determines that a child as defined by Section 22.011(c), Penal Code, was the victim of the offense, by requiring as a condition of parole or mandatory supervision that the releasee:

(1) not:

(A) supervise or participate in any program that includes as participants or recipients persons who are 17 years of age or younger and that regularly provides athletic, civic, or cultural activities; or

(B) go in, on, or within a distance specified by the panel of premises where children commonly gather, including a school, day-care facility, playground, public or private youth center, public swimming pool, or video arcade facility; and

(2) attend for a period of time determined necessary by the panel psychological counseling sessions for sex offenders with an individual or organization that provides sex offender treatment or counseling as specified by the parole officer supervising the releasee after release.

(b-1) Notwithstanding Subsection (b)(1)(B), a requirement that a releasee not go in, on, or within a distance specified by a parole panel of certain premises does not apply to a releasee while the releasee is in or going immediately to or from:

(1) a parole office;

(2) premises at which the releasee is participating in a program or activity required as a condition of release;

(3) a residential facility in which the releasee is required to reside as a condition of release;

(4) a private residence in which the releasee is required to reside as a condition of release; or

(5) any other premises, facility, or location that is:

(A) designed to rehabilitate or reform the releasee; or

(B) authorized by the division as a premises, facility, or location where it is reasonable and necessary for the releasee to be present and at which the releasee has legitimate business, including a church, synagogue, or other established place of religious worship, a workplace, a health care facility, or a location of a funeral.

(c) A parole officer who under Subsection (b)(2) specifies a sex offender treatment provider to provide counseling to a releasee shall:

(1) contact the provider before the releasee is released;

(2) establish the date, time, and place of the first session between the releasee and the provider; and

(3) request the provider to immediately notify the officer if the releasee fails to attend the first session or any subsequent scheduled session.

(d) At any time after the imposition of a condition under Subsection (b)(1), the releasee may request the parole panel to modify the child safety zone applicable to the releasee because the zone as created by the panel:

(1) interferes with the releasee's ability to attend school or hold a job and consequently constitutes an undue hardship for the releasee; or

(2) is broader than necessary to protect the public, given the nature and circumstances of the offense.

(e) A parole officer supervising a releasee may permit the releasee to enter on an event-by-event basis into the child safety zone that the releasee is otherwise prohibited from entering if:

(1) the releasee has served at least two years of the period of supervision imposed on release;

(2) the releasee enters the zone as part of a program to reunite with the releasee's family;

(3) the releasee presents to the parole officer a written proposal specifying:

(A) where the releasee intends to go within the zone;

(B) why and with whom the releasee is going; and

(C) how the releasee intends to cope with any stressful situations that occur;

(4) the sex offender treatment provider treating the releasee agrees with the officer that the releasee should be allowed to attend the event; and

(5) the officer and the treatment provider agree on a chaperon to accompany the releasee, and the chaperon agrees to perform that duty.

(f) In this section, "playground," "premises," "school," "video arcade facility," and "youth center" have the meanings assigned by Section 481.134, Health and Safety Code.

Added by Acts 1997, 75th Leg., ch. 165, Sec. 12.01, eff. Sept. 1, 1997.
Amended by Acts 2001, 77th Leg., ch. 978, Sec. 2, eff. Sept. 1, 2001.

Amended by:

Acts 2007, 80th Leg., R.S., Ch. 593 (H.B. 8), Sec. 3.41, eff. September 1, 2007.

Acts 2011, 82nd Leg., R.S., Ch. 515 (H.B. 2014), Sec. 3.03, eff. September 1, 2011.

Acts 2017, 85th Leg., R.S., Ch. 997 (H.B. 1111), Sec. 1, eff. September 1, 2017.

Sec. 508.188. COMMUNITY SERVICE FOR CERTAIN RELEASEES. A parole panel shall require as a condition of parole or mandatory supervision that a releasee for whom the court has made an affirmative finding under Article 42.014, Code of Criminal Procedure, perform not less than 300 hours of community service at a project designated by the parole panel that primarily serves the person or group that was the target of the releasee.

Added by Acts 1997, 75th Leg., ch. 165, Sec. 12.01, eff. Sept. 1, 1997.

Sec. 508.189. PAROLE FEE FOR CERTAIN RELEASEES. (a) A parole panel shall require as a condition of parole or mandatory supervision that a releasee convicted of an offense under Section 21.02, 21.08, 21.11, 22.011, 22.021, 25.02, 43.25, or 43.26, Penal Code, pay to the division a parole supervision fee of $5 each month during the period of parole supervision.

(b) The division shall send fees collected under this section to the comptroller. The comptroller shall deposit the fees in the general revenue fund to the credit of the sexual assault program fund established under Section 44.0061, Health and Safety Code.

Added by Acts 1997, 75th Leg., ch. 165, Sec. 12.01, eff. Sept. 1, 1997.
Amended by:

Acts 2007, 80th Leg., R.S., Ch. 593 (H.B. 8), Sec. 3.42, eff. September 1, 2007.

Sec. 508.190. AVOIDING VICTIM OF STALKING OFFENSE. (a) A parole panel shall require as a condition of parole or mandatory supervision that a releasee serving a sentence for an offense under Section 42.072, Penal Code, not:

(1) communicate directly or indirectly with the victim;

(2) go to or near the residence, place of employment, or business of the victim; or

(3) go to or near a school, day-care facility, or similar facility where a dependent child of the victim is in attendance.

(b) If a parole panel requires the prohibition contained in Subsection (a)(2) or (3) as a condition of parole or mandatory supervision, the parole panel shall specifically describe the prohibited locations and the minimum distances, if any, that the releasee must maintain from the locations.

Added by Acts 1999, 76th Leg., ch. 62, Sec. 10.26, eff. Sept. 1, 1999.

Sec. 508.191. NO CONTACT WITH VICTIM. (a) If a parole panel releases a defendant on parole or to mandatory supervision, the panel shall require as a condition of parole or mandatory supervision that the defendant not intentionally or knowingly communicate directly or indirectly with a victim of the offense or intentionally or knowingly go near a residence, school, place of employment, or business of a victim. At any time after the defendant is released on parole or to mandatory supervision, a victim of the offense may petition the panel for a modification of the conditions of the defendant's parole or mandatory supervision allowing the defendant contact with the victim subject to reasonable restrictions.

(b) Notwithstanding Subsection (a), a defendant may participate in victim-offender mediation authorized by Section 508.324 on the request of the victim or a guardian of the victim or a close relative of a deceased victim.

(c) In this section, "victim" has the meaning assigned by Article 56A.001, Code of Criminal Procedure.

Added by Acts 1999, 76th Leg., ch. 62, Sec. 10.27, eff. Sept. 1, 1999.
Amended by:

Acts 2019, 86th Leg., R.S., Ch. 469 (H.B. 4173), Sec. 2.48, eff. January 1, 2021.

Sec. 508.192. REENTRY INTO THE UNITED STATES PROHIBITED. (a) In this section, "illegal criminal alien" has the meaning assigned by Section 493.015.

(b) A parole panel shall require as a condition of parole or mandatory supervision that an illegal criminal alien released to the custody of United States Immigration and Customs Enforcement:

(1) regardless of whether a final order of deportation is issued with reference to the illegal criminal alien, leave the United States as soon as possible after release; and

(2) not unlawfully return to or unlawfully reenter the United States in violation of the Immigration Reform and Control Act of 1986 (8 U.S.C. Section 1101 et seq.).

Added by Acts 2011, 82nd Leg., R.S., Ch. 1025 (H.B. 2734), Sec. 1, eff.

September 1, 2011.

SUBCHAPTER G. DISCRETIONARY CONDITIONS OF PAROLE OR MANDATORY SUPERVISION

Sec. 508.221. CONDITIONS PERMITTED GENERALLY. A parole panel may impose as a condition of parole or mandatory supervision any condition that a court may impose on a defendant placed on community supervision under Chapter 42A, Code of Criminal Procedure, including the condition that a releasee submit to testing for controlled substances or submit to electronic monitoring if the parole panel determines that without testing for controlled substances or participation in an electronic monitoring program the inmate would not be released on parole.

Added by Acts 1997, 75th Leg., ch. 165, Sec. 12.01, eff. Sept. 1, 1997.
Amended by:

Acts 2015, 84th Leg., R.S., Ch. 770 (H.B. 2299), Sec. 2.55, eff. January 1, 2017.

Sec. 508.222. PAYMENT OF CERTAIN DAMAGES. A parole panel may require as a condition of parole or mandatory supervision that a releasee make payments in satisfaction of damages for which the releasee is liable under Section 500.002.

Added by Acts 1997, 75th Leg., ch. 165, Sec. 12.01, eff. Sept. 1, 1997.

Sec. 508.223. PSYCHOLOGICAL COUNSELING. A parole panel may require as a condition of parole or mandatory supervision that a releasee serving a sentence for an offense under Section 42.072, Penal Code, attend psychological counseling sessions of a type and for a duration as specified by the parole panel, if the parole panel determines in consultation with a local mental health services provider that appropriate mental health services are available through the Department of State Health Services in accordance with Section 534.053, Health and Safety Code, or through another mental health services provider.

Added by Acts 1997, 75th Leg., ch. 165, Sec. 12.01, eff. Sept. 1, 1997.
Amended by Acts 1999, 76th Leg., ch. 62, Sec. 10.28, eff. Sept. 1, 1999.
Amended by:

Acts 2023, 88th Leg., R.S., Ch. 30 (H.B. 446), Sec. 5.17, eff. September 1, 2023.

Sec. 508.224. SUBSTANCE ABUSE COUNSELING. A parole panel may require as a condition of parole or mandatory supervision that the releasee attend counseling sessions for substance abusers or participate in substance abuse treatment services in a program or facility approved or licensed by the Texas Commission on Alcohol and Drug Abuse if:

(1) the releasee was sentenced for an offense involving a controlled substance; or

(2) the panel determines that the releasee's substance abuse was related to the commission of the offense.

Added by Acts 1997, 75th Leg., ch. 165, Sec. 12.01, eff. Sept. 1, 1997.

Sec. 508.225. CHILD SAFETY ZONE. (a) If the nature of the offense for which an inmate is serving a sentence warrants the establishment of a child safety zone, a parole panel may establish a child safety zone applicable to an inmate serving a sentence for an offense listed in Article 42A.054(a), Code of Criminal Procedure, or for which the judgment contains an affirmative finding under Article 42A.054(c) or (d), Code of Criminal Procedure, by requiring as a condition of parole or release to mandatory supervision that the inmate not:

(1) supervise or participate in any program that includes as participants or recipients persons who are 17 years of age or younger and that regularly provides athletic, civic, or cultural activities; or

(2) go in or on, or within a distance specified by the panel of, a premises where children commonly gather, including a school, day-care facility, playground, public or private youth center, public swimming pool, or video arcade facility.

(a-1) Notwithstanding Subsection (a)(2), a requirement that an inmate not go in, on, or within a distance specified by a parole panel of certain premises does not apply to an inmate while the inmate is in or going immediately to or from:

(1) a parole office;

(2) premises at which the inmate is participating in a program or activity required as a condition of release;

(3) a residential facility in which the inmate is required to reside as a condition of release;

(4) a private residence in which the inmate is required to reside as a condition of release; or

(5) any other premises, facility, or location that is:

(A) designed to rehabilitate or reform the inmate; or

(B) authorized by the division as a premises, facility, or location where it is reasonable and necessary for the inmate to be present and at which the inmate has legitimate business, including a church, synagogue, or other established place of religious worship, a workplace, a health care facility, or a location of a funeral.

(b) At any time after the imposition of a condition under Subsection (a), the inmate may request the parole panel to modify the child safety zone applicable to the inmate because the zone as created by the panel:

(1) interferes with the ability of the inmate to attend school or hold a job and consequently constitutes an undue hardship for the inmate; or

(2) is broader than is necessary to protect the public, given the nature and circumstances of the offense.

(c) This section does not apply to an inmate described by Section 508.187.

(d) In this section, "playground," "premises," "school," "video arcade facility," and "youth center" have the meanings assigned by Section 481.134, Health and Safety Code.

Added by Acts 1999, 76th Leg., ch. 56, Sec. 2, eff. Sept. 1, 1999.
Amended by:

Acts 2015, 84th Leg., R.S., Ch. 770 (H.B. 2299), Sec. 2.56, eff. January 1, 2017.

Acts 2017, 85th Leg., R.S., Ch. 997 (H.B. 1111), Sec. 2, eff. September 1, 2017.

Sec. 508.226. ORCHIECTOMY AS CONDITION PROHIBITED. A parole panel may not require an inmate to undergo an orchiectomy as a condition of release on parole or to mandatory supervision.

Added by Acts 1999, 76th Leg., ch. 62, Sec. 10.29, eff. Sept. 1, 1999.
Renumbered from Sec. 508.225 by Acts 2001, 77th Leg., ch. 1420, Sec. 21.001(45), eff. Sept. 1, 2001.

Sec. 508.227. ELECTRONIC MONITORING OF CERTAIN MEMBERS OF CRIMINAL STREET GANG. (a) This section applies only to a releasee who:

(1) is identified as a member of a criminal street gang in an intelligence database established under Chapter 67, Code of Criminal Procedure; and

(2) has three or more times been convicted of, or received a grant of deferred adjudication community supervision or another functionally equivalent form of community supervision or probation for, a felony offense under the laws of this state, another state, or the United States.

(b) A parole panel may require as a condition of release on parole or to mandatory supervision that a releasee described by Subsection (a) submit to tracking under an electronic monitoring service or other appropriate technological service designed to track a person's location.

Added by Acts 2009, 81st Leg., R.S., Ch. 1130 (H.B. 2086), Sec. 20, eff. September 1, 2009.
Amended by:
Acts 2017, 85th Leg., R.S., Ch. 1058 (H.B. 2931), Sec. 4.12, eff. January 1, 2019.

Sec. 508.228. SEX OFFENDER TREATMENT. A parole panel may require as a condition of release on parole or to mandatory supervision that a releasee participate in a sex offender treatment program as specified by the parole panel if:

(1) the releasee:

(A) was serving a sentence for an offense under Chapter 21, Penal Code; or

(B) is required to register as a sex offender under Chapter 62, Code of Criminal Procedure; or

(2) a designated agent of the board after conducting a hearing that allows the releasee to contest the evidence, on evidence that a sex offense occurred during the commission of the offense for which the releasee was serving a sentence, makes an affirmative finding that, regardless of the offense for which the releasee was serving a sentence, the releasee constitutes a threat to society because of the releasee's lack of sexual control.

Added by Acts 2015, 84th Leg., R.S., Ch. 1114 (H.B. 3387), Sec. 2, eff. September 1, 2015.

SUBCHAPTER H. WARRANTS

Sec. 508.251. ISSUANCE OF WARRANT OR SUMMONS. (a) In a case of parole or mandatory supervision, the director or a designated agent of the director or, in another case, the board on order by the governor, may issue a warrant as provided by Section 508.252 for the return of:

(1) a releasee;

(2) an inmate released although not eligible for release;

(3) a resident released to a preparole or work program;

(4) an inmate released on emergency reprieve or on emergency absence under escort; or

(5) a person released on a conditional pardon.

(b) A warrant issued under Subsection (a) must require the return of the person to the institution from which the person was paroled or released.

(c) Instead of the issuance of a warrant under this section, the division:

(1) may issue to the person a summons requiring the person to appear for a hearing under Section 508.281 if the person:

(A) is not a releasee who is:

(i) on intensive supervision or superintensive supervision;

(ii) an absconder; or

(iii) determined by the division to be a threat to public safety; or

(B) is charged only with committing a new offense that is alleged to have been committed after the first anniversary of the date the person was released on parole or to mandatory supervision if:

(i) the new offense is a Class C misdemeanor under the Penal Code, other than an offense committed against a child younger than 17 years of age or an offense involving family violence, as defined by Section 71.004, Family Code;

(ii) the person has maintained steady employment for at least one year;

(iii) the person has maintained a stable residence for at least one year; and

(iv) the person has not previously been charged with an offense after the person was released on parole or to mandatory supervision; and

(2) shall issue to the person a summons requiring the person to appear for a hearing under Section 508.281 if the person:

(A) is charged only with committing an administrative violation of release that is alleged to have been committed after the first anniversary of the date the person was released on parole or to mandatory supervision;

(B) is not serving a sentence for, and has not been previously convicted of, an offense listed in or described by Article 62.001(5), Code of Criminal Procedure; and

(C) is not a releasee with respect to whom a summons may not be issued under Subdivision (1).

(c-1) A summons issued under Subsection (c) must state the time, date, place, and purpose of the hearing.

(d) A designated agent of the director acts independently from a parole officer and must receive specialized training as determined by the director.

Added by Acts 1997, 75th Leg., ch. 165, Sec. 12.01, eff. Sept. 1, 1997.
Amended by Acts 2003, 78th Leg., ch. 264, Sec. 1, eff. Sept. 1, 2003.
Amended by:

Acts 2011, 82nd Leg., R.S., Ch. 546 (H.B. 2735), Sec. 1, eff. September 1, 2011.

Acts 2015, 84th Leg., R.S., Ch. 693 (H.B. 710), Sec. 1, eff. September 1, 2015.

Sec. 508.252. GROUNDS FOR ISSUANCE OF WARRANT OR SUMMONS. A warrant or summons may be issued under Section 508.251 if:

(1) there is reason to believe that the person has been released although not eligible for release;

(2) the person has been arrested for an offense;

(3) there is a document that is self-authenticating as provided by Rule 902, Texas Rules of Evidence, stating that the person violated a rule or condition of release; or

(4) there is reliable evidence that the person has exhibited behavior during the person's release that indicates to a reasonable person that the person poses a danger to society that warrants the person's immediate return to custody.

Added by Acts 1997, 75th Leg., ch. 165, Sec. 12.01, eff. Sept. 1, 1997. Amended by Acts 1999, 76th Leg., ch. 62, Sec. 10.30, eff. Sept. 1, 1999; Acts 2003, 78th Leg., ch. 264, Sec. 2, eff. Sept. 1, 2003.

Sec. 508.253. EFFECT ON SENTENCE AFTER ISSUANCE OF WARRANT. If it appears a releasee has violated a condition or provision of the releasee's parole or mandatory supervision, the date of the issuance of the warrant to the date of the releasee's arrest is not counted as a part of the time served under the releasee's sentence.

Added by Acts 1997, 75th Leg., ch. 165, Sec. 12.01, eff. Sept. 1, 1997.

Sec. 508.254. DETENTION UNDER WARRANT. (a) A person who is the subject of a warrant may be held in custody pending a determination of all facts surrounding the alleged offense, violation of a rule or condition of release, or dangerous behavior.

(b) A warrant authorizes any officer named by the warrant to take custody of the person and detain the person until a parole panel orders the return of the person to the institution from which the person was released.

(c) Except as provided by Subsection (d), pending a hearing on a charge of parole violation, ineligible release, or violation of a condition of mandatory supervision, a person returned to custody shall remain confined.

(d) A magistrate of the county in which the person is held in custody may release the person on bond pending the hearing if:

(1) the person is arrested or held in custody only on a charge that the person committed an administrative violation of release;

(2) the division, in accordance with Subsection (e), included notice on the warrant for the person's arrest that the person is eligible for release on bond; and

(3) the magistrate determines that the person is not a threat to public safety.

(e) The division shall include a notice on the warrant for the person's arrest indicating that the person is eligible for release on bond under Subsection (d) if the division determines that the person:

(1) has not been previously convicted of:

(A) an offense under Chapter 29, Penal Code;

(B) an offense under Title 5, Penal Code, punishable as a felony; or

(C) an offense involving family violence, as defined by Section 71.004, Family Code;

(2) is not on intensive supervision or super-intensive supervision;

(3) is not an absconder; and

(4) is not a threat to public safety.

(f) The provisions of Chapters 17 and 22, Code of Criminal Procedure, apply to a person released under Subsection (d) in the same manner as those provisions apply to a person released pending an appearance before a court or magistrate, except that the release under that subsection is conditioned on the person's appearance at a hearing under this subchapter.

Added by Acts 1997, 75th Leg., ch. 165, Sec. 12.01, eff. Sept. 1, 1997.
Amended by:

Acts 2015, 84th Leg., R.S., Ch. 472 (S.B. 790), Sec. 1, eff. September 1, 2015.

Sec. 508.255. STATUS AS FUGITIVE FROM JUSTICE. (a) After the issuance of a warrant, a person for whose return a warrant was issued is a fugitive from justice.

(b) The law relating to the right of the state to extradite a person and return a fugitive from justice and Article 42.11, Code of Criminal Procedure, relating to the waiver of all legal requirements to obtain extradition of a fugitive from justice from another state to this state, are not impaired by this chapter and remain in full force and effect.

Added by Acts 1997, 75th Leg., ch. 165, Sec. 12.01, eff. Sept. 1, 1997.

Sec. 508.256. WITHDRAWAL OF WARRANT. At any time before setting a revocation hearing date under Section 508.282, the division may withdraw a warrant and continue supervision of a releasee.

Added by Acts 1997, 75th Leg., ch. 165, Sec. 12.01, eff. Sept. 1, 1997.

SUBCHAPTER I. HEARINGS AND SANCTIONS

Sec. 508.281. HEARING. (a) A releasee, a person released although ineligible for release, or a person granted a conditional pardon is entitled to a hearing before a parole panel or a designated agent of the board under the rules adopted by the board and within a period that permits a parole panel, a designee of the board, or the department to dispose of the charges within the periods established by Sections 508.282(a) and (b) if the releasee or person:

(1) is accused of a violation of the releasee's parole or mandatory supervision or the person's conditional pardon, on information and complaint by a peace officer or parole officer; or

(2) is arrested after an ineligible release.

(b) If a parole panel or designated agent of the board determines that a releasee or person granted a conditional pardon has been convicted of a felony offense committed while an administrative releasee and has been sentenced to a term of confinement in a penal institution, the determination is considered to be a sufficient hearing to revoke the parole or mandatory supervision or recommend to the governor revocation of a conditional pardon without further hearing, except that the parole panel or designated agent shall conduct a hearing to consider mitigating circumstances if requested by the releasee or person granted a conditional pardon.

Text of subsection as amended by Acts 2015, 84th Leg., R.S., Ch. 472 (S.B. 790), Sec. 2

(c) If a designated agent of the board determines that a releasee who appears in compliance with a summons has violated a condition of release, the agent shall notify the board. After the board or a parole panel makes a final determination regarding the violation, the division may issue a warrant requiring the releasee to be held in a county jail pending the return of the releasee to the institution from which the releasee was released.

Text of subsection as amended by Acts 2015, 84th Leg., R.S., Ch. 693 (H.B. 710), Sec. 2

(c) If a hearing before a designated agent of the board is held under this section for a releasee who appears in compliance with a summons, the sheriff of the county in which the releasee is required to appear shall provide the designated agent with a place at the county jail to hold the hearing. After the board or a parole panel makes a final determination that a releasee has violated a condition of release, a warrant may be issued requiring the releasee to be held in the county jail pending:

(1) transfer to an intermediate sanction facility; or

(2) the return of the releasee to the institution from which the releasee was released.

(d) If a parole panel or designated agent of the board determines that a releasee has violated a condition of release required under Section 508.192 and confirms the violation with a peace officer or other law enforcement officer of this state who is authorized under federal law to verify a person's immigration status or, in accordance with 8 U.S.C. Section 1373(c), with a federal law enforcement officer, the determination is considered to be a sufficient hearing to revoke the parole or mandatory supervision without further hearing or determination, except that the parole panel or designated agent shall conduct a hearing to consider mitigating circumstances, if requested by the releasee.

(e) A parole panel or designated agent of the board may not revoke the parole or mandatory supervision of a releasee if the parole panel or designated agent finds that the only evidence supporting the alleged violation of a condition of release is the uncorroborated results of a polygraph examination.

(f) Any hearing required to be conducted by a parole panel under this chapter may be conducted by a designated agent of the board. The designated agent may make recommendations to a parole panel that has responsibility for making a final determination.

Added by Acts 1997, 75th Leg., ch. 165, Sec. 12.01, eff. Sept. 1, 1997. Amended by Acts 1999, 76th Leg., ch. 62, Sec. 10.31, eff. Sept. 1, 1999; Acts 2003, 78th Leg., ch. 264, Sec. 3, eff. Sept. 1, 2003; Acts 2003, 78th Leg., 3rd C.S., ch. 3, Sec. 11.20, eff. Jan. 11, 2004.

Amended by:

Acts 2011, 82nd Leg., R.S., Ch. 1025 (H.B. 2734), Sec. 2, eff. September

1, 2011.

Acts 2013, 83rd Leg., R.S., Ch. 1154 (S.B. 213), Sec. 19, eff. September 1, 2013.

Acts 2013, 83rd Leg., R.S., Ch. 1160 (S.B. 358), Sec. 3, eff. June 14, 2013.

Acts 2015, 84th Leg., R.S., Ch. 472 (S.B. 790), Sec. 2, eff. September 1, 2015.

Acts 2015, 84th Leg., R.S., Ch. 693 (H.B. 710), Sec. 2, eff. September 1, 2015.

Acts 2015, 84th Leg., R.S., Ch. 1236 (S.B. 1296), Sec. 21.001(25), eff. September 1, 2015.

Sec. 508.2811. PRELIMINARY HEARING. A parole panel or a designee of the board shall provide within a reasonable time to an inmate or person described by Section 508.281(a) a preliminary hearing to determine whether probable cause or reasonable grounds exist to believe that the inmate or person has committed an act that would constitute a violation of a condition of release, unless the inmate or person:

(1) waives the preliminary hearing; or

(2) after release:

(A) has been charged only with an administrative violation of a condition of release; or

(B) has been adjudicated guilty of or has pleaded guilty or nolo contendere to an offense committed after release, other than an offense punishable by fine only involving the operation of a motor vehicle, regardless of whether the court has deferred disposition of the case, imposed a sentence in the case, or placed the inmate or person on community supervision.

Added by Acts 1999, 76th Leg., ch. 62, Sec. 10.32, eff. Sept. 1, 1999.

Sec. 508.282. DEADLINES. (a) Except as provided by Subsection (b), a parole panel, a designee of the board, or the department shall dispose of the charges against an inmate or person described by Section 508.281(a):

(1) before the 41st day after the date on which a warrant issued as provided by Section 508.251 is executed, if the inmate or person is arrested only on a charge that the inmate or person has committed an administrative violation of a condition of release; or

(2) before the 91st day after the date on which a warrant issued as provided by Section 508.251 is executed, if:

(A) the inmate or person allegedly committed an offense after release; and

(B) an indictment, information, or complaint for the offense has not been filed in court.

(b) A parole panel, a designee of the board, or the department is not required to dispose of the charges against an inmate or person within the period required by Subsection (a) if:

(1) the inmate or person is in custody in another state or a federal correctional institution;

(2) the parole panel or a designee of the board is not provided a place by the sheriff to hold the hearing, in which event the department, parole panel, or designee is not required to dispose of the charges against the inmate or person until the 30th day after the date on which the sheriff provides a place to hold the hearing; or

(3) the inmate or person is granted a continuance by a parole panel or a designee of the board in the inmate's or person's hearing under Section 508.281(a), but in no event may a parole panel, a designee of the board, or the department dispose of the charges against the person later than the 15th day after the date on which the parole panel, designee, or department would otherwise be required to dispose of the charges under this section, unless the inmate or person is released from custody and a summons is issued under Section 508.251 requiring the inmate or person to appear for a hearing under Section 508.281.

(c) In Subsections (a), (b), and (f), charges against an inmate or person are disposed of when:

(1) the inmate's or person's conditional pardon, parole, or release to mandatory supervision is:

(A) revoked; or

(B) continued or modified and the inmate or person is released from the county jail;

(2) the warrant for the inmate or person issued under Section 508.251 is withdrawn; or

(3) the inmate or person is transferred to a facility described by Section 508.284 for further proceedings.

(d) A sheriff, not later than the 10th day before the date on which the sheriff intends to release from custody an inmate or person described by Section 508.281(a) or transfer the inmate or person to the custody of an entity other than the department, shall notify the department of the intended release or transfer.

(e) If a warrant for an inmate or person issued under Section 508.251 is withdrawn, a summons may be issued requiring the inmate or person to appear for a hearing under Section 508.281.

(f) A parole panel, a designee of the board, or the department shall dispose of the charges against a releasee for whom a warrant is issued under Section 508.281(c) not later than the 31st day after the date on which the warrant is issued.

Added by Acts 1997, 75th Leg., ch. 165, Sec. 12.01, eff. Sept. 1, 1997. Amended by Acts 1999, 76th Leg., ch. 62, Sec. 10.33, eff. Sept. 1, 1999; Acts 2003, 78th Leg., ch. 264, Sec. 4, eff. Sept. 1, 2003; Acts 2003, 78th Leg., ch. 1194, Sec. 1, eff. Sept. 1, 2003.
Amended by:

Acts 2023, 88th Leg., R.S., Ch. 1055 (S.B. 374), Sec. 1, eff. September 1, 2023.

Sec. 508.283. SANCTIONS. (a) After a parole panel or designated agent of the board has held a hearing under Section 508.281, in any manner warranted by the evidence:

(1) the board may recommend to the governor to continue, revoke, or modify the conditional pardon; and

(2) a parole panel may continue, revoke, or modify the parole or mandatory supervision.

(b) If the parole, mandatory supervision, or conditional pardon of a person described by Section 508.149(a) is revoked, the person may be required to serve the remaining portion of the sentence on which the person was released. The remaining portion is computed without credit for the time from the date of the person's release to the date of revocation.

(c) If the parole, mandatory supervision, or conditional pardon of a person other than a person described by Section 508.149(a) is revoked, the person may be required to serve the remaining portion of the sentence on which the person was released. For a person who on the date of issuance of a warrant or summons initiating the revocation process is subject to a sentence the remaining portion of which is greater than the amount of time from the date of the person's release to the date of issuance of the warrant or summons, the remaining portion is to be served without credit for the time from the date of the person's release to the date of revocation. For a person who on the date of issuance of the warrant or summons is subject to a sentence the remaining portion of which is less than the amount of time from the date of the person's release to the date of issuance of the warrant or summons, the remaining portion is to be served without credit for an amount of time equal to the remaining portion of the sentence on the date of issuance of the warrant or citation.

(d) If a warrant is issued charging a violation of a release condition or a summons is issued for a hearing under Section 508.281, the sentence time credit may be suspended until a determination is made in the case. The suspended time credit may be reinstated if the parole, mandatory supervision, or conditional pardon is continued.

(e) If a person's parole or mandatory supervision is modified after it is established that the person violated conditions of release, the board may require the releasee to remain under custodial supervision in a county jail for a period of not less than 60 days or more than 180 days. A sheriff is required to accept an inmate sanctioned under this subsection only if the commissioners court of the county in which the sheriff serves and the Texas Department of Criminal Justice have entered into a contract providing for the housing of persons sanctioned under this subsection.

Added by Acts 1997, 75th Leg., ch. 165, Sec. 12.01, eff. Sept. 1, 1997. Amended by Acts 1999, 76th Leg., ch. 62, Sec. 10.34, eff. Sept. 1, 1999; Acts 2001, 77th Leg., ch. 856, Sec. 7, eff. Sept. 1, 2001; Acts 2001, 77th Leg., ch. 1197, Sec. 1, eff. Sept. 1, 2001; Acts 2003, 78th Leg., ch. 1275, Sec. 2(62), eff. Sept. 1, 2003.

Sec. 508.284. TRANSFER PENDING REVOCATION HEARING. The department, as provided by Section 508.282(c), may authorize a facility that is otherwise required to detain and house an inmate or person to transfer the inmate or person to a correctional facility operated by the department or under contract with the department if:

(1) the department determines that adequate space is available in the facility to which the inmate or person is to be transferred; and

(2) the facility to which the inmate or person is to be transferred is located not more than 150 miles from the facility from which the inmate or person is to be transferred.

Added by Acts 1999, 76th Leg., ch. 62, Sec. 10.35, eff. Sept. 1, 1999.

SUBCHAPTER J. MISCELLANEOUS

Sec. 508.311. DUTY TO PROVIDE INFORMATION. On request of a member of the board or employee of the board or department, a public official of the state, including a judge, district attorney, county attorney, or police officer, who has information relating to an inmate eligible for parole shall send to the department in writing the information in the official's possession or under the official's control.

Added by Acts 1997, 75th Leg., ch. 165, Sec. 12.01, eff. Sept. 1, 1997.

Sec. 508.312. INFORMATION ON RECIDIVISM OF RELEASEES. The Texas Board of Criminal Justice shall collect information on recidivism of releasees under the supervision of the division and shall use the information to evaluate operations.

Added by Acts 1997, 75th Leg., ch. 165, Sec. 12.01, eff. Sept. 1, 1997.

Sec. 508.313. CONFIDENTIAL INFORMATION. (a) All information obtained and maintained, including a victim protest letter or other correspondence, a victim impact statement, a list of inmates eligible for release on parole, and an arrest record of an inmate, is confidential and privileged if the information relates to:

(1) an inmate of the institutional division subject to release on parole, release to mandatory supervision, or executive clemency;

(2) a releasee; or

(3) a person directly identified in any proposed plan of release for an inmate.

(b) Statistical and general information relating to the parole and mandatory supervision system, including the names of releasees and data recorded relating to parole and mandatory supervision services, is not confidential or privileged and must be made available for public inspection at any reasonable time.

(c) The department, on request or in the normal course of official business, shall provide information that is confidential and privileged under Subsection (a) to:

(1) the governor;

(2) a member of the board or a parole commissioner;

(3) the Criminal Justice Policy Council in performing duties of the council under Section 413.017; or

(4) an eligible entity requesting information for a law enforcement, prosecutorial, correctional, clemency, or treatment purpose.

(d) In this section, "eligible entity" means:

(1) a government agency, including the office of a prosecuting attorney;

(2) an organization with which the department contracts or an organization to which the department provides a grant; or

(3) an organization to which inmates are referred for services by the department.

(e) This section does not apply to information relating to a sex offender that is authorized for release under Chapter 62, Code of Criminal Procedure.

(f) This section does not apply to information that is subject to required public disclosure under Section 552.029.

Added by Acts 1997, 75th Leg., ch. 165, Sec. 12.01, eff. Sept. 1, 1997. Amended by Acts 1999, 76th Leg., ch. 62, Sec. 10.36, eff. Sept. 1, 1999; Acts 1999, 76th Leg., ch. 783, Sec. 3, eff. Aug. 30, 1999; Acts 2001, 77th Leg., ch. 856, Sec. 8, eff. Sept. 1, 2001; Acts 2003, 78th Leg., ch. 6, Sec. 3, eff. April 10, 2003; Acts 2003, 78th Leg., 3rd C.S., ch. 3, Sec. 11.21, eff. Jan. 11, 2004.

Sec. 508.314. ACCESS TO INMATES. The department shall:

(1) grant to a member or employee of the board access at all reasonable times to any inmate;

(2) provide for the member or employee or a representative of the member or employee facilities for communicating with or observing an inmate; and

(3) furnish to the member or employee:

(A) any report the member or employee requires relating to the conduct or character of an inmate; or

(B) other facts a parole panel considers pertinent in determining whether an inmate will be released on parole.

Added by Acts 1997, 75th Leg., ch. 165, Sec. 12.01, eff. Sept. 1, 1997.

Sec. 508.315. ELECTRONIC MONITORING PROGRAMS. (a) To establish and maintain an electronic monitoring program under this chapter, the department may:

(1) fund an electronic monitoring program in a parole office;

(2) develop standards for the operation of an electronic monitoring program in a parole office; and

(3) fund the purchase, lease, or maintenance of electronic monitoring equipment.

(b) In determining whether electronic monitoring equipment should be leased or purchased, the department shall consider the rate at which technological change makes electronic monitoring equipment obsolete.

Added by Acts 1997, 75th Leg., ch. 165, Sec. 12.01, eff. Sept. 1, 1997.

Sec. 508.316. SPECIAL PROGRAMS. (a) The department may contract for services for releasees if funds are appropriated to the department for the services, including services for releasees who have a history of:

(1) mental impairment or intellectual disability;

(2) substance abuse; or

(3) sexual offenses.

(b) The department shall seek funding for a contract under this section as a priority item.

Added by Acts 1997, 75th Leg., ch. 165, Sec. 12.01, eff. Sept. 1, 1997.
Amended by:

Acts 2023, 88th Leg., R.S., Ch. 30 (H.B. 446), Sec. 5.18, eff. September 1, 2023.

Sec. 508.317. INTENSIVE SUPERVISION PROGRAM; SUPER-INTENSIVE SUPERVISION PROGRAM. (a) The department shall establish a program to provide intensive supervision to inmates released under Subchapter B, Chapter 499, and other inmates determined by a parole panel or the department to require intensive supervision.

(b) The Texas Board of Criminal Justice shall adopt rules that establish standards for determining which inmates require intensive supervision.

(c) The program must provide the level of supervision the department provides that is higher than any level of supervision other than the level of supervision described by Subsection (d).

(d) The department shall establish a program to provide super-intensive supervision to inmates released on parole or mandatory supervision and determined by parole panels to require super-intensive supervision. The program must provide the highest level of supervision provided by the department.

Added by Acts 1997, 75th Leg., ch. 165, Sec. 12.01, eff. Sept. 1, 1997.
Amended by Acts 1999, 76th Leg., ch. 62, Sec. 10.37, eff. Sept. 1, 1999.

Sec. 508.318. CONTINUING EDUCATION PROGRAM. (a) The Texas Board of Criminal Justice and the Texas Education Agency shall adopt a memorandum of understanding that establishes the respective responsibilities of the board and the agency in implementing a continuing education program to increase the literacy of releasees.

(b) The Texas Board of Criminal Justice and the agency shall coordinate the development of the memorandum of understanding and each by rule shall adopt the memorandum.

Added by Acts 1997, 75th Leg., ch. 165, Sec. 12.01, eff. Sept. 1, 1997.

Sec. 508.319. PROGRAM TO ASSESS AND ENHANCE EDUCATIONAL AND VOCATIONAL SKILLS. (a) The department, with the assistance of public school districts, community and public junior colleges, public and private institutions of higher education, and other appropriate public and private entities, may establish a developmental program based on information obtained under Section 508.183 for an inmate to be released to the supervision of the division.

(b) The developmental program may provide the inmate with the educational and vocational training necessary to:

(1) meet the average skill level required under Section 508.183; and

(2) acquire employment while in the custody of the division to lessen the likelihood that the inmate will return to the institutional division.

(c) To decrease state expense for a program established under this section, the Texas Workforce Commission shall provide to the department and the other entities described by Subsection (a) information relating to obtaining financial assistance under applicable programs of public or private entities.

(d) The department may establish a developmental program similar to the program described by Subsection (a) for inmates released from the institutional division who will not be supervised by the department.

Added by Acts 1997, 75th Leg., ch. 165, Sec. 12.01, eff. Sept. 1, 1997.

Sec. 508.320. CONTRACTS FOR LEASE OF FEDERAL FACILITIES. (a) The department may contract with the federal government for the lease of a military base or other federal facility that is not being used by the federal government.

(b) The department may use a facility leased under this section to house releasees in the custody of the division.

(c) The department may not enter into a contract under this section unless funds have been appropriated specifically to make payments on a contract under this section.

(d) The department shall attempt to enter into contracts that will provide the department with facilities located in various parts of the state.

Added by Acts 1997, 75th Leg., ch. 165, Sec. 12.01, eff. Sept. 1, 1997.

Sec. 508.321. REPORTING, MANAGEMENT, AND COLLECTION SERVICES. The department, with the approval of the Texas Board of Criminal Justice, may contract with a public or private vendor to provide telephone reporting, automated caseload management, or collection services for:

(1) fines, fees, restitution, or other costs ordered to be paid by a court; or

(2) fees collected by the division.

Added by Acts 1997, 75th Leg., ch. 165, Sec. 12.01, eff. Sept. 1, 1997.

Sec. 508.322. RELEASEE RESTITUTION FUND. (a) The releasee restitution fund is a fund outside the treasury and consists of restitution payments made by releasees. Money in the fund may be used only to pay restitution as required by a condition of parole or mandatory supervision to victims of criminal offenses.

(b) The comptroller is the trustee of the releasee restitution fund as provided by Section 404.073.

(c) When a parole panel orders the payment of restitution from a releasee as provided by Article 42.037(h), Code of Criminal Procedure, the department shall:

(1) collect the payment for disbursement to the victim;

(2) deposit the payment in the releasee restitution fund; and

(3) transmit the payment to the clerk of the court that entered the order of restitution as soon as practicable for the clerk to remit the payment to the victim.

(c-1) The department shall include the releasee's name and other relevant identifying information, the cause number, and the payment amount when transmitting a payment to the clerk of the court under Subsection (c)(3).

(c-2) On receipt of a payment transmitted to the clerk of the court under Subsection (c)(3), the clerk shall process and account for the payment in the same manner as if the payment had been made directly to the clerk.

(d) If a victim who is entitled to restitution cannot be located, immediately after receiving a final payment in satisfaction of an order of restitution for the victim, the clerk of the court shall attempt to notify the victim of that fact by certified mail, mailed to the last known address of the victim. If a victim then makes a claim for payment, the clerk of the court promptly shall remit the payment to the victim.

(e) If a victim who is entitled to restitution does not make a claim for payment before the fifth anniversary of the date the clerk of the court receives the initial restitution payment or if, after the victim makes a claim for payment, the clerk is unable to locate the victim for a period of five years after the date the clerk last made a payment to the victim, any unclaimed restitution payments being held by the clerk for payment to the victim are presumed abandoned. The clerk of the court shall report and deliver to the comptroller all unclaimed restitution payments presumed abandoned under this section in the manner provided by Chapter 77, Property Code.

(f) If on March 1 a clerk of the court is not holding unclaimed restitution payments that are presumed abandoned under this section, the clerk shall file a property report under Section 77.051, Property Code, that certifies that the clerk is not holding any unclaimed restitution payments that are presumed abandoned under this section.

Added by Acts 1997, 75th Leg., ch. 165, Sec. 12.01, eff. Sept. 1, 1997.
Amended by Acts 2001, 77th Leg., ch. 856, Sec. 9, eff. Sept. 1, 2001.
Amended by:

Acts 2017, 85th Leg., R.S., Ch. 351 (H.B. 1866), Sec. 3, eff. September 1, 2017.

Acts 2023, 88th Leg., R.S., Ch. 864 (H.B. 3603), Sec. 1, eff. December 1, 2023.

Sec. 508.323. AUDIT. The financial transactions of the division and the board are subject to audit by the state auditor in accordance with Chapter 321.

Added by Acts 1997, 75th Leg., ch. 165, Sec. 12.01, eff. Sept. 1, 1997.

Sec. 508.324. VICTIM-OFFENDER MEDIATION. If the pardons and paroles division receives notice from the victim services office of the department that a victim of the defendant, or the victim's guardian or close relative, wishes to participate in victim-offender mediation with a person released on parole or to mandatory supervision, the division shall cooperate and assist the person if the person chooses to participate in the mediation program provided by the office. The pardons and paroles division may not require the defendant to participate and may not reward the person for participation by modifying conditions of release or the person's level of supervision or by granting any other benefit to the person.

Added by Acts 1999, 76th Leg., ch. 62, Sec. 10.38, eff. Sept. 1, 1999.

The Texas Board of Pardons and Paroles

Parole Guidelines Annual Report FY 2021

Published by:
The Texas Board of Pardons and Paroles

David Gutiérrez
Chair and Presiding Officer
P. O. Box 13401
Capitol Station
Austin, Texas 78711

March 2022

TABLE OF CONTENTS

MISSION AND VISION STATEMENTS 2

INTRODUCTION 3

HISTORY OF TEXAS PAROLE GUIDELINES 5

COMPONENTS OF THE GUIDELINES 7

- Risk Assessment Instrument 7
  - Static Factors 7
  - Dynamic Factors 7
- Offense Severity Class 7

THE PAROLE GUIDELINES SCORE 8

ACTUAL APPROVAL RATES FY 2021 9

- Guidelines Level Statewide, Approval Rate by Guidelines Level 9
- Guidelines Level by Regional Office .... 10 - 16
  - Amarillo Board Office 10
  - Angleton Board Office 11
  - Austin Board Office 12
  - Gatesville Board Office 13
  - Huntsville Board Office 14
  - Palestine Board Office 15
  - San Antonio Board Office 16

MISSION STATEMENT

The mission of the Texas Board of Pardons and Paroles is to perform its duties as imposed by Article 4, Section 11, of the Texas Constitution and:

- Determine which prisoners are to be released on parole or discretionary mandatory supervision;
- Determine conditions of parole and mandatory supervision;
- Determine revocation of parole and mandatory supervision; and
- Recommend the resolution of clemency matters to the Governor.

VISION STATEMENT

The Texas Board of Pardons and Paroles, guided by sound application of the discretionary authority vested by the Constitution of the State of Texas, shall:

- Render just determination in regard to parole release and revocations, thereby maximizing the restoration of human potential while restraining the growth of prison and jail populations;
- Impose reasonable and prudent conditions of release consistent with the goal of structured reintegration of the releasee into the community; and
- Resolutely administer the clemency process with recommendations to the Governor fully commensurate with public safety and due consideration.

INTRODUCTION

In accordance with Section 508.1445, Government Code, the Texas Board of Pardons and Paroles (Board) annually shall submit a report to the Criminal Justice Legislative Oversight Committee, the Lieutenant Governor, the Speaker of the House of Representatives, and the presiding officers of the standing committees in the Senate and House of Representatives primarily responsible for criminal justice regarding the Board's application of the Parole Guidelines adopted under Section 508.144.

The information in this report was obtained from the Texas Department of Criminal Justice who is responsible for maintaining and providing statistical information relating to parole and mandatory supervision pursuant to Government Code Section 508.313(b).

Board Rule 145.2 Standard Parole Guidelines:

(a) The parole panels are vested with complete discretion in making parole decisions to accomplish the mandatory duties found in Chapter 508, Government Code.

(b) Parole guidelines have been adopted by the Board to assist parole panels in the selection of possible candidates for release. Parole guidelines are applied as a basis, but not as the exclusive criteria, upon which parole panels base release decisions.

(1) The parole guidelines consist of a risk assessment instrument and an offense severity scale. Combined, these components serve as an instrument to guide parole release decisions.

(2) The risk assessment instrument includes two sets of components, static and dynamic factors.

(A) Static factors include:

(i) Age at first admission to a juvenile or adult correctional facility;

(ii) History of supervisory release revocations for felony offenses;

(iii) Prior incarcerations;

(iv) Employment history; and

(v) The commitment offense.

(B) Dynamic factors include:

(i) The offender's current age;

(ii) Whether the offender is a confirmed security threat group (gang) member;

(iii) Education, vocational and certified on-the-job training programs completed during the present incarceration;

(iv) Prison disciplinary conduct; and

(v) Current prison custody level.

(3) Scores from the risk assessment instrument are combined with an offense severity rating for the sentenced offense of record to determine a parole candidate's guidelines level.

(c) The adoption and use of the parole guidelines does not imply the creation of any parole release formula, or a right or expectation by an offender to parole based upon the guidelines. The risk assessment instrument and the offense severity scale, while utilized for research and reporting, are not to be construed so as to mandate either a favorable or unfavorable parole decision. The parole guidelines serve as an aid in the parole decision process and the parole decision shall be at the discretion of the Board and the voting parole panel.

(d) The Board is authorized to revise the parole guidelines as warranted.

The Board guidelines combine a research-based risk assessment of the offender with a measurement of the severity of the offense. The risk assessment measures the likelihood of an offender to have a successful parole. It uses both an offender's historical (Static) information and current (Dynamic) situation.

The assessed level of risk combines with the offense severity ranking to create a Parole Guidelines Score. The score ranges from 1, for an individual with the poorest probability of success, to 7, for an offender with the greatest probability of success.

While the Board seeks to maximize the state's ability to restore human potential to society through the granting of parole, its first priority is always public safety.

The range of Recommended Parole Approval Rates utilized by the Board in this Annual Report was developed by a consultant to the Board in 2001. The range of Recommended Parole Approval Rates were established to monitor its compliance for each category or score within the guidelines.

The Board realizes individual voter and aggregate release decisions may not fall within the Recommended Parole Approval Range. The following explanations are provided for the variations that exist between the Actual Parole Approval Rates for individual parole panel members, regional offices, and the state as a whole, and the range of Recommended Parole Approval Rates.

Board Members and Parole Commissioners vote cases on a daily basis; therefore, at the time of the parole panel member's vote, the current monthly aggregate total by approval rates are not available to them. Additionally, the Parole Guidelines are only one of the tools utilized by the parole panel members when making individual offender discretionary decisions. Other factors the panel members consider include: information from victims and trial officials, judges, district attorneys, sheriffs and police chiefs, the nature of the specific offense, support information, and offenders with short sentences which limit the voting options for placement into a rehabilitative program.

The seven Board offices are primarily situated near high density prison populations. As such, certain units often house a specific type of offender. For example, the Gatesville area houses female offenders, thus the Gatesville Board office votes a higher percentage of female offenders than other Board offices. Other units may house less violent offenders or offenders with shorter sentences. Such differences in unit populations impact the approval percentages of each Board office, so particular attention is warranted when comparing regional approval rates.

HISTORY OF TEXAS PAROLE GUIDELINES

Prior to 1983, the Board used Salient and Significant Factor Score Sheets when making parole decisions. The Salient Factor Score sought to classify parole candidates according to the likelihood for succeeding under parole supervision. The Significant Factor Score reflected the seriousness of the offense committed.

In 1983, the Board adopted the PABLO Scale to aid members in applying similar criteria to parole decisions. The scale calculated the risk of releasing an offender by evaluating the offender's rating on 20 variables, which included criminal history, juvenile history, substance abuse history, age at the time of the offense, education, etc.

In 1985, the Legislature mandated that the Board incorporate Parole Guidelines, with minimum release criteria, into parole decision-making. Based on research, the Parole Guidelines were to consider the seriousness of the offense and the likelihood of a favorable parole outcome.

In 1987, the Board combined the PABLO Scale with Parole Guidelines that measured parole risks to set a parole risk score.

The risk factors consisted of nine variables shown to be associated with recidivism (number of prior convictions, number of prior incarcerations, age at first incarceration, commitment offense, number of prior parole or probation violations, history of alcohol/drug dependence, employment history, level of education, and release plan).

The offender's most severe current offense was assigned one of four severity levels (highest, high, medium, and low). Time served was used to adjust the risk and offense severity score. Based on the score, the Board would set a tentative parole date that still could be overridden by the Board at its discretion. However, the reasons for overrides had to conform to a limited set of factors established by the Board.

In 1993, the 73rd Legislature directed the Criminal Justice Policy Council (CJPC) to report "at least annually to the Legislative Criminal Justice Board, the Texas Board of Criminal Justice and the Texas Board of Pardons and Paroles on the use of the Parole Guidelines by each member of the Board in making parole decisions."

In 1996, after conducting a study of guideline usage, CJPC recommended revised guidelines be developed to ensure that the criteria reflect Board policy, to apply the guidelines in a consistent manner to all candidates for parole (reliable), and to predict the risk to public safety (valid).

Reliability is a measure of the consistency of Institutional Parole Officers (IPOs) in extracting and presenting the same data to the Board for consideration in parole decisions. Validity is a measure of risk factors to accurately predict whether a candidate is a good, moderate, or poor risk to succeed on parole. Parole Guidelines accomplish these two objectives by developing scoring instruments that use well-defined measures of risk that correlate with post-release success.

In 1998, the Board applied to the National Institute of Corrections (NIC) for technical assistance in developing revised Parole Guidelines that would provide both reliability and validity.

After agreeing to an initial site visit and assessment, NIC reported, "...to simply update existing guidelines will not increase the viability or effectiveness of the Board's case decision making and would not bring Texas in line with new approaches that have been successful in other jurisdictions. A fundamental re-examination and redesign is required."

In 1999, the Board contracted with Security Response Technologies, Inc. (SRT, Inc.), an 18-month, three-phase project:

- Phase I - A comprehensive review of the Board's current practices as well as those of other states in using Parole Guidelines.

- Phase II - A validation test of existing guidelines, along with an evaluation of other selected factors to be used in assessing risk.
- Phase III - Training of Board Members, Parole Commissioners, and IPOs in using the new guidelines.

On January 18, 2001, the Policy Board adopted the assessment and design of the new Parole Guidelines as submitted by SRT, Inc.

On July 1, 2001, the IPOs began calculating a Parole Guidelines Score for each eligible offender using the new guidelines.

On September 1, 2001, the Board panels began using the new Parole Guidelines to assist in making parole decisions.

The Board continued to assess and review the guidelines through its Parole Guidelines Committee.

On May 15, 2006, the Board requested a voting pattern analysis on DWI offender cases. Dr. James Austin, NIC consultant, presented a report based on data re-validating the Board's Parole Guidelines and risk analysis.

On January 29, 2009, the Board adopted Dr. Austin's report, modifying and updating the Parole Guidelines. Additionally, he revised instructions for completing the risk assessment, created a new Supplemental DWI Risk Assessment Factors and Scale, and trained staff.

In 2010, the Board selected MGT of America, Inc., to conduct research and provide recommendations for updating the Parole Guidelines.

The 18-month initiative researched data on domestic violence, gender (female) differences, and security threat group considerations.

In 2012, the consultant conducted research and provided recommendations for updating the Parole Guidelines. The consultant recommended no changes in factors involving domestic violence and security threat groups but did recommend a change to separate risk scales by gender, which the Board adopted.

On January 16, 2014, Dr. Austin presented a report based on data re-validation of the Board's Parole Guideline Levels. Based on Dr. Austin's report and recommendations, in June 2014, the Chair requested technical assistance from the Bureau of Justice (BOJ) National Training and Technical Center. The BOJ awarded the Board a grant for technical assistance involving the Board's Parole Guidelines in October 2014. Dr. Austin began working with the Board in December 2014 to examine and suggest modifications as appropriate to the Board's estimated Approval Rates and Parole Guideline Levels.

On April 16, 2015, the Board partnered with a consultant from the Bureau of Justice Assistance and adopted a new range of Recommended Parole Approval Rates. The adjustments were made based on new data and evidence-based practices that have emerged since the initial range of Recommended Parole Approval Rates were established in 2001. In addition and based upon research, a recommendation was also made to change the final guideline level from 4 to 3 in the "High" Risk, "Moderate" Offense Severity position of the Matrix. With implementation of these changes, the Board anticipates individual votes and aggregate release decisions will fall between the new ranges and the variations between Actual Parole Approval Rates and Recommended Parole Approval Rates will decrease.

On October 28, 2020, the Board adopted Dr. James Austin's re-validation report, enhancing the risk assessment instrument, and discontinued use of the Supplemental DWI Risk Assessment Factors and Scale.

Periodically, various new custody level codes are added to the Texas Department of Criminal Justice Classification and Records system. The result of adding these new codes affects the "Custody Level Conversion Chart" the IPOs use to calculate the Overall Parole Guidelines Score. As new codes were added during 2016, programming was and will be in the future completed and implemented as necessary.

COMPONENTS OF THE GUIDELINES

The Parole Guidelines consist of two major components that interact to provide a single score. The first is a Risk Assessment Instrument that weighs both the static and dynamic factors associated with the offender's record. The second component is Offense Severeity Class.

RISK ASSESSMENT INSTRUMENT

Static factors come from the offender's prior criminal record, which do not change over time.

Static factors include:

- Age at first commitment to a juvenile or adult correctional facility;
- History of supervisory release revocations for felony offenses;
- Prior incarcerations;
- Employment history; and
- The commitment offense.

Dynamic factors reflect characteristics the offender has demonstrated since being incarcerated and can change over time.

Dynamic factors include:

- Current age;
- Whether the offender is a confirmed security threat group (gang) member;
- Education, vocational, and certified on-the-job training programs completed during the present incarceration;
- Prison disciplinary conduct; and
- Current prison custody level.

An offender receives 0-10 points on Static Factors and 0-9 points on Dynamic Factors. A low score is associated with low risk. The higher the score, the greater the risk in granting parole.

As a result of the re-validation study completed in 2012, it was determined that a separate risk scale for males and females was necessary.

SCORE ASSIGNED RISK LEVEL

Based on total of Static and Dynamic Factor points, risk level assigned to

Offense Severity Class	MALE (POINTS)	FEMALE (POINTS)
Low Risk	3 or less	5 or less
Moderate Risk	4-6	6-9
High Risk	7-9	10+
Highest Risk	10+	N/A

OFFENSE SEVERITY CLASS

The Board has assigned an Offense Severity Ranking to each of the felony offenses in the statute.

Offense Severity Classes range from Low, for non-violent crimes such as credit card abuse, to Highest, for capital murder. If an offender is incarcerated for more than one offense, the most serious active offense is assigned an Offense Severity Class identified by the established list.

The Board's Parole Guidelines Committee continually reviews current offenses for possible re-ranking and new offenses for appropriate ranking.

THE PAROLE GUIDELINES SCORE

The two components of the guidelines – Risk Assessment and Offense Severity – are merged into a matrix that creates the offender's Parole Guidelines Score (at the intersection of risk level and offense severity in the diagrams below). Separate risk scales have been developed for male and female offenders.

Parole Guidelines Scores range from 1, for an individual with the poorest probability of success, to 7, for an offender with the greatest probability of success.

The guidelines are not automatic nor is the Parole Guideline Score presumptive of whether an offender will be paroled. Parole panel members retain the discretion to vote outside the guidelines when circumstances of an individual case merit doing so.

Offense Severity Class	MALE RISK LEVEL				FEMALE RISK LEVEL		
	Highest (10+)	High (7-9)	Moderate (4-6)	Low (3 or less)	High (10+)	Moderate (6-9)	Low (5 or less)
Highest	1	2	2	3	2	2	3
High	2	3	4	4	3	4	4
Moderate	2	3	5	6	3	5	6
Low	3	4	6	7	4	6	7

ACTUAL APPROVAL RATES FY 2021

GUIDELINES LEVEL STATEWIDE

GUIDELINE LEVEL	CASES CONSIDERED	CASES APPROVED	APPROVAL RATE	RECOMMENDED APPROVAL RATE
1	99	9	9.09%	0% - 20%
2	5,426	1,577	29.06%	15% - 35%
3	6,732	2,434	36.16%	25% - 40%
4	23,104	7,437	32.19%	30% - 45%
5	15,140	5,708	37.70%	35% - 50%
6	11,645	5,860	50.32%	45% - 70%
7	3,329	2,152	64.64%	65% - 100%
TOTAL	**65,475**	**25,177**	**38.45%**	

(Total Parole Considerations in FY 2021 were 65,488 with 13 MRIS cases considered and approved without a guidelines score)

Board Members and Parole Commissioners vote cases daily. A report is generated on a monthly basis, reflecting the range of recommended approval rates by guideline level. It is important to note that the panel members are unaware of the aggregate approval rates during the voting process, which means they are unable to determine if the vote is within the range of recommended approval rates. The parole panel members provide approval and denial reasons for all votes.

A Notice of Parole Panel Action letter is generated with a detailed written statement explaining the denial reason(s) specific to each case. The IPO delivers a copy of the notice to the offender.

It should be noted the approval rate for Parole Guideline Level 7 (64.64%) is below the recommended approval rate of 65%. The maximum difference was less than 1%. The Board is continually evaluating the severity of offenses and making adjustments as deemed appropriate.

On a monthly basis, parole panel members are provided statistical information regarding their votes for each guideline level so they may compare their approval rates to the recommended approval rates. However, as previously noted with this report, panel members consider other factors in addition to a parole guidelines score, which may impact approval scores for each guideline score.

APPROVAL RATE BY GUIDELINE LEVEL

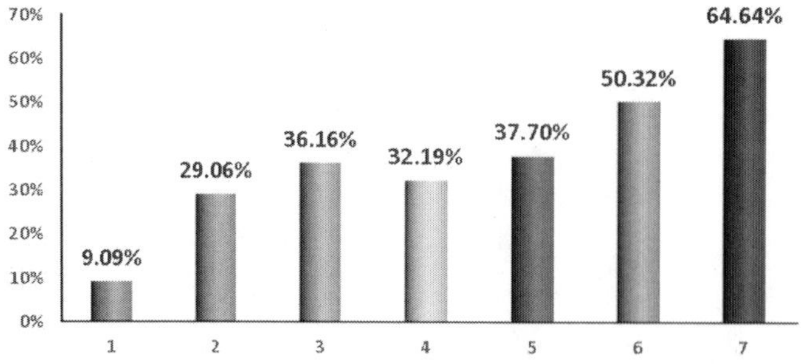

GUIDELINES LEVEL BY BOARD MEMBER/PAROLE COMMISSIONER GROUPED BY BOARD OFFICE

The statutory requirements to report Parole Guidelines votes by regional offices are displayed in the following charts grouped by Board office.

Vacancies and new parole panel voters are noted in footnotes. Occasionally a Board Member or Parole Commissioner is out of the office for an extended period of time and a panel member from another office will vote cases in their absence.

AMARILLO BOARD OFFICE

James LaFavers, Board Member

LEVEL	CASES CONSIDERED	CASES APPROVED	APPROVAL RATE	RECOMMENDED APPROVAL RATE
1	13	4	30.77%	0% - 20%
2	1,101	478	43.42%	15% - 35%
3	1,922	1,071	55.72%	25% - 40%
4	3,006	1,305	43.41%	30% - 45%
5	1,420	608	42.82%	35% - 50%
6	920	488	53.04%	45% - 70%
7	210	105	50.00%	65% - 100%
TOTAL	**8,592**	**4,059**	**47.24%**	

Elodia Brito, Parole Commissioner

LEVEL	CASES CONSIDERED	CASES APPROVED	APPROVAL RATE	RECOMMENDED APPROVAL RATE
1	16	4	25.00%	0% - 20%
2	721	240	33.29%	15% - 35%
3	668	236	35.33%	25% - 40%
4	2,483	862	34.72%	30% - 45%
5	1,520	653	42.96%	35% - 50%
6	938	510	54.37%	45% - 70%
7	228	144	63.16%	65% - 100%
TOTAL	**6,574**	**2,649**	**40.30%**	

Jeffrey Marton, Parole Commissioner*

LEVEL	CASES CONSIDERED	CASES APPROVED	APPROVAL RATE	RECOMMENDED APPROVAL RATE
1	7	1	14.29%	0% - 20%
2	146	35	23.97%	15% - 35%
3	150	49	32.67%	25% - 40%
4	468	136	29.06%	30% - 45%
5	271	113	41.70%	35% - 50%
6	164	69	42.07%	45% - 70%
7	58	27	46.55%	65% - 100%
TOTAL	**1,264**	**430**	**34.02%**	

**Jeffrey Marton served as a Parole Commissioner from June 1, 2021, to August 31, 2021.*

ANGLETON BOARD OFFICE

Carmella Jones, Board Member

LEVEL	CASES CONSIDERED	CASES APPROVED	APPROVAL RATE	RECOMMENDED APPROVAL RATE
1	5	0	0.00%	0% - 20%
2	834	371	44.48%	15% - 35%
3	1,684	998	59.26%	25% - 40%
4	2,847	1,249	43.87%	30% - 45%
5	1,639	704	42.95%	35% - 50%
6	1,320	718	54.39%	45% - 70%
7	383	264	68.93%	65% - 100%
TOTAL	**8,712**	**4,304**	**49.40%**	

Ira Evans, Parole Commissioner

LEVEL	CASES CONSIDERED	CASES APPROVED	APPROVAL RATE	RECOMMENDED APPROVAL RATE
1	5	0	0.00%	0% - 20%
2	512	168	32.81%	15% - 35%
3	533	175	32.83%	25% - 40%
4	2,608	814	31.21%	30% - 45%
5	1,808	723	39.99%	35% - 50%
6	1,638	892	54.46%	45% - 70%
7	541	374	69.13%	65% - 100%
TOTAL	**7,645**	**3,146**	**41.15%**	

Raymond Gonzalez, Parole Commissioner

LEVEL	CASES CONSIDERED	CASES APPROVED	APPROVAL RATE	RECOMMENDED APPROVAL RATE
1	6	0	0.00%	0% - 20%
2	453	157	34.66%	15% - 35%
3	501	171	34.13%	25% - 40%
4	2,297	802	34.92%	30% - 45%
5	1,628	712	43.73%	35% - 50%
6	1,486	854	57.47%	45% - 70%
7	468	332	70.94%	65% - 100%
TOTAL	**6,839**	**3,028**	**44.28%**	

AUSTIN BOARD OFFICE

Ed Robertson, Board Member

LEVEL	CASES CONSIDERED	CASES APPROVED	APPROVAL RATE	RECOMMENDED APPROVAL RATE
1	4	0	0.00%	0% - 20%
2	601	312	51.91%	15% - 35%
3	1,666	984	59.06%	25% - 40%
4	2,384	1,060	44.46%	30% - 45%
5	1,187	363	30.58%	35% - 50%
6	1,218	420	34.48%	45% - 70%
7	371	171	46.09%	65% - 100%
TOTAL	**7,431**	**3,310**	**44.54%**	

Troy Fox, Parole Commissioner

LEVEL	CASES CONSIDERED	CASES APPROVED	APPROVAL RATE	RECOMMENDED APPROVAL RATE
1	3	0	0.00%	0% - 20%
2	193	72	37.31%	15% - 35%
3	335	115	34.33%	25% - 40%
4	1,698	579	34.10%	30% - 45%
5	1,175	377	32.09%	35% - 50%
6	1,177	526	44.69%	45% - 70%
7	370	228	61.62%	65% - 100%
TOTAL	**4,951**	**1,897**	**38.32%**	

Marsha Moberley, Parole Commissioner

LEVEL	CASES CONSIDERED	CASES APPROVED	APPROVAL RATE	RECOMMENDED APPROVAL RATE
1	1	0	0.00%	0% - 20%
2	178	58	32.58%	15% - 35%
3	367	155	42.23%	25% - 40%
4	1,657	554	33.43%	30% - 45%
5	1,149	402	34.99%	35% - 50%
6	1,194	564	47.24%	45% - 70%
7	378	269	71.16%	65% - 100%
TOTAL	**4,924**	**2,002**	**40.66%**	

GATESVILLE BOARD OFFICE

David Gutiérrez, Chair

LEVEL	CASES CONSIDERED	CASES APPROVED	APPROVAL RATE	RECOMMENDED APPROVAL RATE
1	0	0	N/A	0% - 20%
2	243	175	72.02%	15% - 35%
3	857	719	83.90%	25% - 40%
4	695	489	70.36%	30% - 45%
5	198	90	45.45%	35% - 50%
6	196	129	65.82%	45% - 70%
7	94	75	79.79%	65% - 100%
TOTAL	**2,283**	**1,677**	**73.46%**	

Lee Anne Eck-Massingill, Parole Commissioner

LEVEL	CASES CONSIDERED	CASES APPROVED	APPROVAL RATE	RECOMMENDED APPROVAL RATE
1	13	2	15.38%	0% - 20%
2	463	148	31.97%	15% - 35%
3	624	219	35.10%	25% - 40%
4	2,880	993	34.48%	30% - 45%
5	2,302	885	38.44%	35% - 50%
6	2,156	1,136	52.69%	45% - 70%
7	761	543	71.35%	65% - 100%
TOTAL	**9,199**	**3,926**	**42.68%**	

Roel Tejada, Parole Commissioner

LEVEL	CASES CONSIDERED	CASES APPROVED	APPROVAL RATE	RECOMMENDED APPROVAL RATE
1	13	2	15.38%	0% - 20%
2	453	147	32.45%	15% - 35%
3	599	213	35.56%	25% - 40%
4	2,815	1,011	35.91%	30% - 45%
5	2,250	880	39.11%	35% - 50%
6	2,097	1,123	53.55%	45% - 70%
7	733	534	72.85%	65% - 100%
TOTAL	**8,960**	**3,910**	**43.64%**	

HUNTSVILLE BOARD OFFICE

A. D'Wayne Jernigan, Board Member

LEVEL	CASES CONSIDERED	CASES APPROVED	APPROVAL RATE	RECOMMENDED APPROVAL RATE
1	14	0	0.00%	0% - 20%
2	1,045	330	31.58%	15% - 35%
3	1,824	924	50.66%	25% - 40%
4	2,953	1,006	34.07%	30% - 45%
5	1,449	440	30.37%	35% - 50%
6	954	379	39.73%	45% - 70%
7	258	150	58.14%	65% - 100%
TOTAL	**8,497**	**3,229**	**38.00%**	

Roy (Tony) Garcia, Parole Commissioner*

LEVEL	CASES CONSIDERED	CASES APPROVED	APPROVAL RATE	RECOMMENDED APPROVAL RATE
1	6	0	0.00%	0% - 20%
2	497	102	20.52%	15% - 35%
3	427	104	24.36%	25% - 40%
4	1,859	491	26.41%	30% - 45%
5	1,253	472	37.67%	35% - 50%
6	725	357	49.24%	45% - 70%
7	187	131	70.05%	65% - 100%
TOTAL	**4,954**	**1,657**	**33.45%**	

Tracy Long, Parole Commissioner

LEVEL	CASES CONSIDERED	CASES APPROVED	APPROVAL RATE	RECOMMENDED APPROVAL RATE
1	10	0	0.00%	0% - 20%
2	634	121	19.09%	15% - 35%
3	591	136	23.01%	25% - 40%
4	2,343	577	24.63%	30% - 45%
5	1,452	571	39.33%	35% - 50%
6	972	469	48.25%	45% - 70%
7	235	166	70.64%	65% - 100%
TOTAL	**6,237**	**2,040**	**32.71%**	

Mary J. Farley, Parole Commissioner**

LEVEL	CASES CONSIDERED	CASES APPROVED	APPROVAL RATE	RECOMMENDED APPROVAL RATE
1	15	1	6.67%	0% - 20%
2	693	227	32.76%	15% - 35%
3	646	241	37.31%	25% - 40%
4	2,429	846	34.83%	30% - 45%
5	1,481	628	42.40%	35% - 50%
6	1,034	551	53.29%	45% - 70%
7	235	130	55.32%	65% - 100%
TOTAL	**6,533**	**2,624**	**40.17%**	

**Roy (Tony) Garcia served as a Parole Commissioner through May 31, 2021.*
***Mary Farley served as a Parole Commissioner at the Amarillo Board office from September 1, 2020, to May 31, 2021, and at the Huntsville Board office from June 1, 2021, to August 31, 2021.*

PALESTINE BOARD OFFICE

Brian Long, Board Member

LEVEL	CASES CONSIDERED	CASES APPROVED	APPROVAL RATE	RECOMMENDED APPROVAL RATE
1	20	0	0.00%	0% - 20%
2	957	293	30.62%	15% - 35%
3	1,925	923	47.95%	25% - 40%
4	2,940	1,110	37.76%	30% - 45%
5	1,339	606	45.26%	35% - 50%
6	935	535	57.22%	45% - 70%
7	242	166	68.60%	65% - 100%
TOTAL	**8,358**	**3,633**	**43.47%**	

Wanda Saliagas, Parole Commissioner

LEVEL	CASES CONSIDERED	CASES APPROVED	APPROVAL RATE	RECOMMENDED APPROVAL RATE
1	12	0	0.00%	0% - 20%
2	567	102	17.99%	15% - 35%
3	541	139	25.69%	25% - 40%
4	2,118	486	22.95%	30% - 45%
5	1,233	425	34.47%	35% - 50%
6	835	402	48.14%	45% - 70%
7	226	124	54.87%	65% - 100%
TOTAL	5,532	**1,678**	**30.33%**	

James Kiel, Parole Commissioner

LEVEL	CASES CONSIDERED	CASES APPROVED	APPROVAL RATE	RECOMMENDED APPROVAL RATE
1	10	0	0.00%	0% - 20%
2	560	99	17.68%	15% - 35%
3	545	164	30.09%	25% - 40%
4	2,267	650	28.67%	30% - 45%
5	1,333	575	43.14%	35% - 50%
6	914	527	57.66%	45% - 70%
7	225	163	72.44%	65% - 100%
TOTAL	**5,854**	**2,178**	**37.21%**	

SAN ANTONIO BOARD OFFICE

Fred Solis, Board Member*

LEVEL	CASES CONSIDERED	CASES APPROVED	APPROVAL RATE	RECOMMENDED APPROVAL RATE
1	3	0	0.00%	0% - 20%
2	467	209	44.75%	15% - 35%
3	878	494	56.26%	25% - 40%
4	1,541	616	39.97%	30% - 45%
5	974	234	24.02%	35% - 50%
6	530	207	39.06%	45% - 70%
7	82	30	36.59%	65% - 100%
TOTAL	**4,475**	**1,790**	**40.00%**	

Linda Molina, Board Member**

LEVEL	CASES CONSIDERED	CASES APPROVED	APPROVAL RATE	RECOMMENDED APPROVAL RATE
1	11	3	27.27%	0% - 20%
2	366	149	40.71%	15% - 35%
3	703	427	60.74%	25% - 40%
4	1,375	560	40.73%	30% - 45%
5	751	247	32.89%	35% - 50%
6	532	232	43.61%	45% - 70%
7	179	63	35.20%	65% - 100%
TOTAL	**3,917**	**1,681**	**42.92%**	

Charles Speier, Parole Commissioner

LEVEL	CASES CONSIDERED	CASES APPROVED	APPROVAL RATE	RECOMMENDED APPROVAL RATE
1	6	1	16.67%	0% - 20%
2	453	138	30.46%	15% - 35%
3	402	133	33.08%	25% - 40%
4	2,108	686	32.54%	30% - 45%
5	1,552	533	34.34%	35% - 50%
6	1,013	473	46.69%	45% - 70%
7	228	98	42.98%	65% - 100%
TOTAL	**5,762**	**2,062**	**35.79%**	

Anthony Ramirez, Parole Commissioner

LEVEL	CASES CONSIDERED	CASES APPROVED	APPROVAL RATE	RECOMMENDED APPROVAL RATE
1	14	1	7.14%	0% - 20%
2	455	125	27.47%	15% - 35%
3	423	129	30.50%	25% - 40%
4	2,185	653	29.89%	30% - 45%
5	1,644	487	29.62%	35% - 50%
6	1,023	411	40.18%	45% - 70%
7	223	106	47.53%	65% - 100%
TOTAL	**5,967**	**1,912**	**32.04%**	

**Fred Solis served as a Board Member through April 2, 2021.*
***Linda Molina served as a Board Member from April 5, 2021 to August 31, 2021*

Cover and back page photo courtesy of Wenling01 | Dreamstime.com

The Texas Board of Pardons and Paroles
P.O. Box 14301 • Capitol Station

Austin, Texas 78711

(512) 406-5452

www.tdcj.texas.gov/bpp

The Texas Board of Pardons and Paroles

Annual Statistical Report FY 2022

MISSION STATEMENT

THE MISSION OF THE TEXAS BOARD OF PARDONS AND PAROLES is to perform its duties as imposed by Article 4, Section 11, of the Texas Constitution and:

- Determine which prisoners are to be released on parole or discretionary mandatory supervision;
- Determine conditions of parole and mandatory supervision;
- Determine revocation of parole and mandatory supervision; and
- Recommend the resolution of clemency matters to the Governor.

VISION STATEMENT

THE TEXAS BOARD OF PARDONS AND PAROLES, guided by sound application of the discretionary authority vested by the Constitution of the State of Texas, shall:

- Render just determination in regard to parole release and revocations, thereby maximizing the restoration of human potential while restraining the growth of prison and jail populations;
- Impose reasonable and prudent conditions of release consistent with the goal of structured reintegration of the releasee into the community; and
- Resolutely administer the clemency process with recommendations to the Governor fully commensurate with public safety and due consideration.

In accordance with Section 508.036(a)(5), Government Code, the Presiding Officer shall report at least annually to the Governor and the Legislature on the activities of the Board and Parole Commissioners.

The information in this report was obtained from the Texas Department of Criminal Justice, which is responsible for maintaining and providing statistical information relating to parole and mandatory supervision pursuant to Section 508.313(b), Government Code.

TABLE OF CONTENTS

REPORT OVERVIEW 2

PAROLE REVIEW PROCESS 4

SUMMARY OF BOARD ACTIVITY 5

Parole 5

Discretionary Mandatory Supervision 9

MEDICALLY RECOMMENDED INTENSIVE SUPERVISION (MRIS) 11

SPECIAL REVIEW 12

OTHER VOTES AND ACTIVITIES 13

SUPER INTENSIVE SUPERVISION PROGRAM (SISP) 14

INSTITUTIONAL PAROLE ACTIVITY 15

HEARING/WAIVER ACTIVITY 16

EXECUTIVE CLEMENCY 22

AGENCY EXPENDITURES 24

GLOSSARY OF TERMS 25

REPORT OVERVIEW

The Texas Board of Pardons and Paroles (Board), a constitutionally created agency, decides whether to parole eligible offenders, the terms of parole supervision, and whether to revoke parole if terms are violated. The Board also recommends clemency to the Governor.

The Board consists of seven members appointed for six-year terms by the Governor with the advice and consent of the Senate. Board Members must be representative of the general public and have lived in Texas the two years before appointment. The Presiding Officer reports directly to the Governor and serves as the administrative head of the agency.

The Board sets policy for parole and mandatory supervision consideration, votes special cases requiring a full Board vote, and votes clemency matters.

The Board uses research-based parole guidelines to assess each offender's likelihood for a successful parole against the risk to society.

In deciding whether to revoke parole, the Board uses a graduated sanctions approach. Depending on the seriousness of the violation, the Board may continue parole, impose additional conditions, place the offender in an Intermediate Sanction Facility, or use other alternatives to revoking parole and sending the offender back to prison.

Fifteen Parole Commissioners are hired by the Presiding Officer to assist the Board in deciding parole release and revocation by serving as voting members on parole panels.

David Gutiérrez
Presiding Officer

A. D'Wayne Jernigan

Carmella Jones

James LaFavers

Brian Long

Marsha Moberley

Linda Molina

Ed Robertson

BOARD MEMBERS	APPOINTED	TERM EXPIRES OR EXPIRED	OFFICE
David Gutiérrez	09/14/2009	02/01/2027	Gatesville
A. D'Wayne Jernigan*	01/08/2019	02/01/2025	Huntsville
Carmella Jones**	06/14/2018	02/01/2025	Huntsville
James LaFavers	07/01/2011	02/01/2023	Amarillo
Brian Long	09/27/2017	02/01/2023	Palestine
Marsha Moberley***	03/25/2022	02/01/2025	Angleton
Linda Molina	03/02/2021	02/01/2027	San Antonio
Ed Robertson	08/31/2015	02/01/2027	Austin

**D'Wayne Jernigan served as a Board Member through October 18, 2021.*
***Carmella Jones served as a Board Member at the Angleton Board office from September 1, 2021, to November 14, 2021, and at the Huntsville Board office from November 15, 2021, to August 31, 2022.*
****Marsha Moberley served as a Parole Commissioner at the Austin Board office from September 1, 2021, to March 31, 2022, and as a Board Member at the Angleton Board office from April 1, 2022, to August 31, 2022.*

The central agency headquarters is in Austin, with offices at:

Price Daniel Building
209 W. 14th St., Suite 500
Austin, Texas 78701

8610 Shoal Creek Boulevard
Austin, Texas 78757

For general information, call: 512-406-5452 or email: bpp_pio@tdcj.texas.gov.

The agency's mailing address is:

Texas Board of Pardons and Paroles
P.O. Box 13401
Austin, TX 78711-3401

Each of the seven Board offices is supervised by a Board Member and includes two Parole Commissioners. Board offices are in:

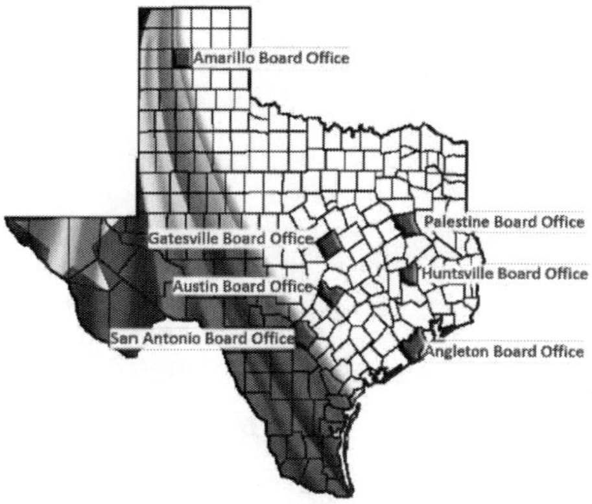

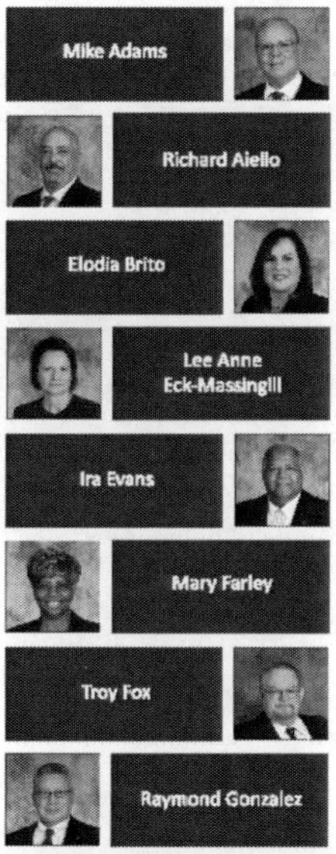

PAROLE COMMISSIONERS	OFFICE
Mike Adams*	Huntsville
Richard Aiello**	Austin
Elodia Brito	Amarillo
Lee Anne Eck-Massingill	Gatesville
Ira Evans	Angleton
Mary Farley***	Austin
Troy Fox	Austin
Raymond Gonzalez	Angleton

PAROLE COMMISSIONERS	OFFICE
James Paul Kiel	Palestine
Tracy Long	Huntsville
Jeffrey Marton	Amarillo
Anthony Ramirez	San Antonio
Wanda Saliagas	Palestine
Charles Speier	San Antonio
Roel Tejada	Gatesville

**Michael Adams served as a Parole Commissioner from June 1, 2022, to August 31, 2022.*
***Richard Aiello served as a Parole Commissioner from June 1, 2022, to August 31, 2022.*
****Mary Farley served as a Parole Commissioner at the Huntsville Board office from September 1, 2021, to May 1, 2022, and at the Austin Board office from May 2, 2022, to August 31, 2022.*

PAROLE REVIEW PROCESS

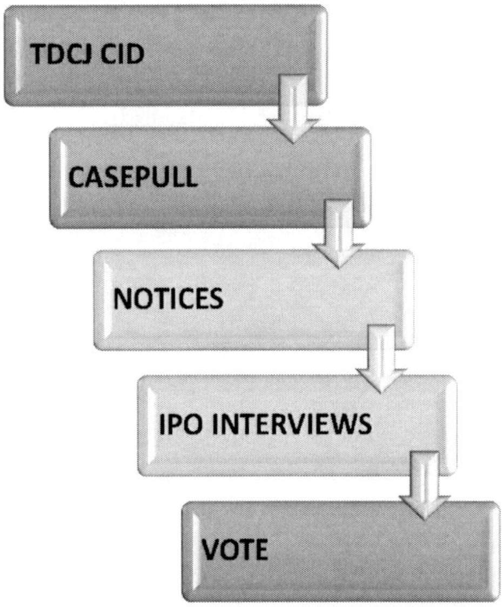

The parole review process entails an exhaustive review and consideration of an offender's case, including, but not limited to, conviction offense, medical and psychological history, and how the offender has adjusted and behaved in prison. Case files arrive regularly in each Board office or are sent as an electronic file through the Offender Information Management System (OIMS). Each parole panel of the Board reviews files and interviews victims upon request as required in Section 508.153, Government Code. Interviews with offenders and other individuals in support or protest of an offender are at the discretion of the parole panel's lead voter.

Parole Panels

A parole panel is composed of one Board Member and two Parole Commissioners who make decisions by majority vote concerning parole and discretionary mandatory release, revocation, and imposing conditions of supervision. For offenders convicted of certain offenses, the law requires a vote of two-thirds of the Board Members to grant parole (Section 508.046, Government Code).

Parole Review

All offenders sentenced to a term of incarceration in the Texas Department of Criminal Justice Correctional Institutions Division (TDCJ CID) are eligible for release on parole, except those sentenced to death or life imprisonment without parole.

If an offender is denied parole, the Board is required to set a future date for parole reconsideration. If the offender is not convicted of an offense listed in Section 508.149(a), Government Code, this date must be set as soon as practical after the first anniversary of the denial date. If the offender is serving a sentence for an offense listed in Section 508.149(a), Government Code, or an offense punishable as a felony of the second or third degree under Section 22.04, Penal Code, the date may be set up to five years from the denial date. If the offender is serving a sentence under Section 22.021, Penal Code, or a life sentence for a capital felony, the date may be set up to ten years from the denial date.

Board Activity Report

The Board was established by the Texas Constitution to make decisions concerning parole and to recommend clemency to the Governor. The tables in this section of the annual report detail the activities of the Board Members and Parole Commissioners, including votes for and against parole and discretionary mandatory supervision, revocation and non-revocation decisions, the number of hearings conducted and waivers reviewed, and the number of clemency cases reviewed by the Board Members.

Parole Considerations

The overall parole approval rate for FY 2022 was 39.32 percent *(see table on page 5)*. Parole considerations in the following table are separated into violent and non-violent and aggravated sexual and aggravated non-sexual cases. An example of a violent offense is murder and a non-violent offense is credit-debit card fraud. The sexual and non-sexual categories are self-explanatory.

Additional tables in this section provide a history of the overall parole approval rates, approval and denial rates for each Board Member, approval rate by type, and other related parole tables by designated categories, i.e., Consecutive Sentences, Parole in Absentia, Medically Recommended Intensive Supervision (MRIS), and Special Review.

SUMMARY OF BOARD ACTIVITY

Parole Considerations and Approval Rates by Offense Type

	CASES CONSIDERED	CASES APPROVED	APPROVAL RATE
Violent Aggravated Non-Sexual	10,725	4,389	40.92%
Violent Aggravated Sexual	3,499	1,424	40.70%
Violent Non-Aggravated Non-Sexual	11,413	3,617	31.69%
Non-Aggravated Sexual	1,930	673	34.87%
Non-Violent	35,012	14,501	41.42%
TOTALS	**62,579**	**24,604**	**39.32%**

Parole Approval Rates by Offense Type

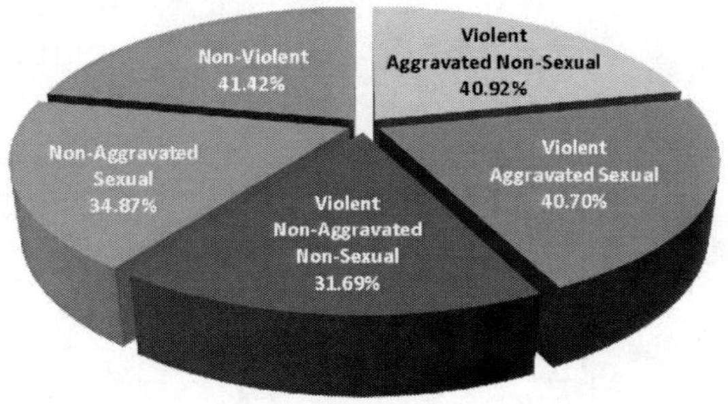

Parole Approval Rates
15-Year Trend

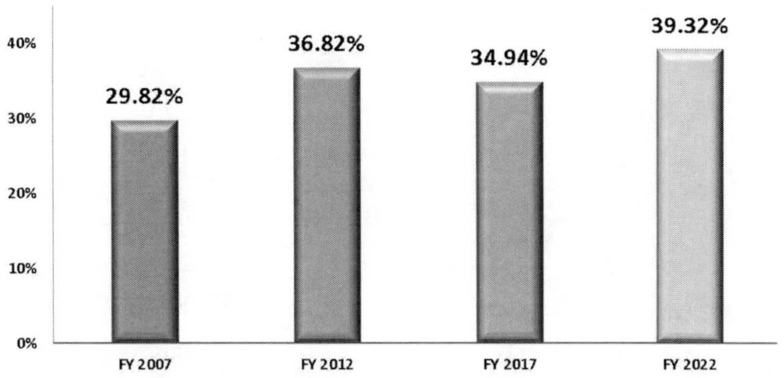

Parole Considerations and Approval Rates History FY 2018 - FY 2022

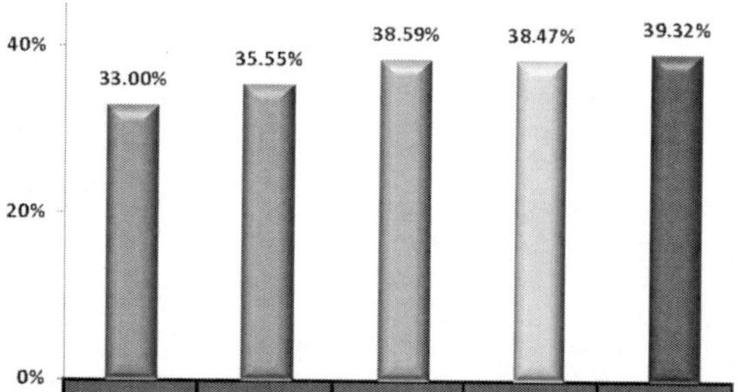

	FY 2018	FY 2019	FY 2020	FY 2021	FY 2022
Cases Considered	80,495	78,346	77,530	65,488	62,579
Cases Approved	26,566	27,855	29,919	25,190	24,604
Approval Rate	33.00%	35.55%	38.59%	38.47%	39.32%

Parole Considerations by Board Members and Parole Commissioners

	TOTAL VOTES	NUMBER APPROVED	APPROVAL RATE	DENIAL RATE
Adams, R.	2,529	983	38.87%	61.13%
Aiello, R.	1,309	547	41.79%	58.21%
Brito, E.	5,981	2,059	34.43%	65.57%
Eck-Massingill, L.	6,826	3,151	46.16%	53.84%
Evans, I.	7,642	3,179	41.60%	58.40%
Farley, M.	6,385	3,095	48.47%	51.53%
Fox, T.	7,455	2,799	37.55%	62.45%
Gonzalez, R.	7,657	3,195	41.73%	58.27%
Gutierrez, D.	1,500	1,092	72.80%	27.20%
Jernigan, D.	1,358	544	40.06%	59.94%
Jones, C.	7,875	4,092	51.96%	48.04%
Kiel, J.	5,190	1,807	34.82%	65.18%
LaFavers, J.	6,318	2,770	43.84%	56.16%
Long, B.	6,801	2,797	41.13%	58.87%
Long, T.	6,595	2,768	41.97%	58.03%
Marton, J.	6,205	2,018	32.52%	67.48%
Moberley, M.	6,411	2,795	43.60%	56.40%
Molina, L.	7,761	2,859	36.84%	63.16%
Ramirez, A.	6,624	2,290	34.57%	65.43%
Robertson, E.	7,510	3,022	40.24%	59.76%
Saliagas, W.	5,217	1,687	32.34%	67.66%
Speier, C.	5,025	1,845	36.72%	63.28%
Tejada, R.	7,849	3,585	45.67%	54.33%
TOTAL	**134,023**	**54,979**	**41.02%**	**58.98%**

Voting members include 8 Board Members and 15 Parole Commissioners.

Parole Approvals by Voting Options

	VOTING OPTION	TOTAL VOTES	PERCENT
FI-1	Release the offender when eligible.	5,130	20.85%
FI-2 (Mo/Yr)	Release on a specified future date.	4,097	16.65%
FI-3R (Mo/Yr)*	Transfer to a TDCJ rehabilitation program. Release to parole only after program completion and not earlier than three months from specified date. Such TDCJ program may include either CHANGES/Lifeskills, Voyager, Segovia Pre-Release Center (Segovia PRC), or any other approved tier program.	4,007	16.29%
FI-4R (Mo/Yr)*	Transfer to a TDCJ rehabilitation program. Release to parole only after program completion and not earlier than four months from specified date. Such TDCJ program shall be the Sex offender Education Program (SOEP).	693	2.82%
FI-5	Transfer to In-Prison Therapeutic Community Program (IPTC). Release to aftercare component only after completion of IPTC.	3,055	12.42%
FI-6	Transfer to a DWI Program and release to a continuum of care program.	935	3.80%
FI-6R (Mo/Yr)*	Transfer to a TDCJ rehabilitation program. Release to parole only after completion and no earlier than six months from specified date. Such TDCJ program may include the Pre-Release Therapeutic Community (PRTC), Pre-Release Substance Abuse Program (PRSAP), or In-Prison Therapeutic Community Program (IPTC), or any other approved tier program.	5,187	21.08%
FI-7R (Mo/Yr)*	Transfer to a TDCJ rehabilitation program. Release to parole only after program completion and not earlier than seven months from the specified date. Such TDCJ program shall be the Serious and Violent Offender Reentry Initiative (SVORI).	105	0.43%
FI-9R (Mo/Yr)*	Transfer to a TDCJ rehabilitation program. Release to parole only after program completion and not earlier than nine months from specified date. Such TDCJ program shall be the Sex Offender Treatment Program (SOTP-9).	1,028	4.18%
FI-18R (Mo/Yr)*	Transfer to a TDCJ rehabilitation treatment program. Release to parole only after program completion and no earlier than 18 months from specified date. Such TDCJ program shall be either the Sex Offender Treatment Program (SOTP-18) or the InnerChange Freedom Initiative (IFI).	79	0.32%
CU/FI (Mo/Yr-Cause No)	Designate the date on which the offender serving consecutive sentences would have been eligible for release on parole if the offender had been sentenced to serve a single sentence. This date shall be within a three-year incarceration period following the panel decision.	288	1.17%
	TOTAL FI VOTES	**24,604**	**100.00%**
	TOTAL TIER VOTES ONLY	**11,099**	**45.11%**

**Rehabilitation tier voting options include various programs within TDCJ CID that must be completed before offenders are released on parole. These rehabilitation programs are designed to help offenders prepare for their return to the community and facilitate their successful reentry into society.*

***The 45.11 percent represents the actual percentage of Rehabilitation Tier Votes (FI-3R, FI-4R, FI-6R, FI-7R, FI-9R, and FI-18R) of the total 24,604 FI votes.*

Consecutive Sentences

An offender who has two or more convictions and is serving consecutive sentences will serve each conviction one after the other. An offender who has two or more convictions and is serving concurrent sentences will serve each conviction at the same time. The court of conviction determines if sentences will be served consecutively or concurrently.

- If all offenses in the series of consecutive sentences occurred on or after September 1, 1987, then each sentence must be considered separately from the other consecutive sentences in the series.
- If approved for parole on the current sentence, the offender will begin serving the next sentence on the date designated by the parole panel.
- On the last and final sentence, the offender is reviewed in the same manner as any offender sentenced to serve a single sentence.
- Offenders are not released until parole is granted or the mandatory release date is reached for the last sentence in the series.

Parole Considerations for Offenders Serving Consecutive Sentences

	PAROLE FROM CID	PIA	TOTALS
Considered	1,079	10	**1,089**
Approved	287	1	**288**
Approval Rate	26.60%	10.00%	**26.45%**

Parole in Absentia (Parole Review and Mandatory Supervision for Offenders Not in Actual Physical Custody of TDCJ CID)

Parole in Absentia (PIA) refers to offenders sentenced to confinement in TDCJ CID but released on Texas parole while incarcerated in a county jail, a facility in another state, or a federal facility.

PIA County of Release

	PAROLE	MS	DMS	TOTALS	PERCENT
Federal Jurisdiction	96	1	49	**146**	53.28%
Other TDCJ Custody	0	0	0	**0**	0.00%
Other State Jurisdiction	13	1	10	**24**	8.76%
Harris County Jail	3	0	9	**12**	4.38%
Bexar County Jail	1	0	10	**11**	4.01%
Brazoria County Jail	2	0	3	**5**	1.82%
Colin County Jail	1	0	4	**5**	1.82%
Dallas County Jail	1	0	4	**5**	1.82%
Tarrant County Jail	1	0	4	**5**	1.82%
Other *	18	0	43	**61**	22.26%
TOTALS	**136**	**2**	**136**	**274**	**100.00%**

** The remainder of county jails and unspecified release sites, each of which had less than 5 PIA releases in FY 2022.*

Discretionary Mandatory Supervision (DMS)

For offenses committed on or after September 1, 1996, a parole panel is required to approve an offender's release to mandatory supervision. A parole panel may deny an offender's release to mandatory supervision when it determines that an offender's accrued good conduct time is not an accurate reflection of the offender's potential for rehabilitation and the offender's release would endanger the public.

Prior to DMS, certain offenders were released to mandatory supervision according to the statutory requirements without a parole panel vote.

Offenders excluded from the mandatory supervision law are those serving a sentence for or previously convicted of any of the following offenses:

- Aggravated Assault, 1st or 2nd Degree
- Aggravated Kidnapping, 1st or 2nd Degree
- Aggravated Robbery, 1st Degree
- Aggravated Sexual Assault, 1st Degree
- Any Offense with an Affirmative Finding of a Deadly Weapon
- Arson, 1st Degree
- Burglary, 1st Degree
- Capital Murder
- Compelling Prostitution
- Continuous Sexual Abuse of Young Child or Children
- Indecency with a Child
- Injury to a Child, Elderly, or Disabled Individual, 1st Degree
- Murder, 1st or 2nd Degree
- Robbery, 2nd Degree
- Sexual Assault
- Sexual Performance by a Child
- Trafficking of Persons
- A Felony Increased Under Health and Safety Code (Drug-Free Zones or Use of Child in Commission of Offense)

DMS Considerations

The overall DMS approval rate is 49.29 percent. DMS votes are listed by considerations and approval rates by offense type, considerations and approval rates history, and considerations by each voting member.

DMS Considerations and Approval Rates by Offense Type

	CASES CONSIDERED	CASES APPROVED	APPROVAL RATE
Violent Aggravated Non-Sexual	18	8	44.44%
Violent Aggravated Sexual	1	0	0.00%
Violent Non-Aggravated Non-Sexual	3,627	1,528	42.13%
Non-Aggravated Sexual	272	118	43.38%
Non-Violent	10,155	5,282	52.01%
TOTALS	**14,073**	**6,936**	**49.29%**

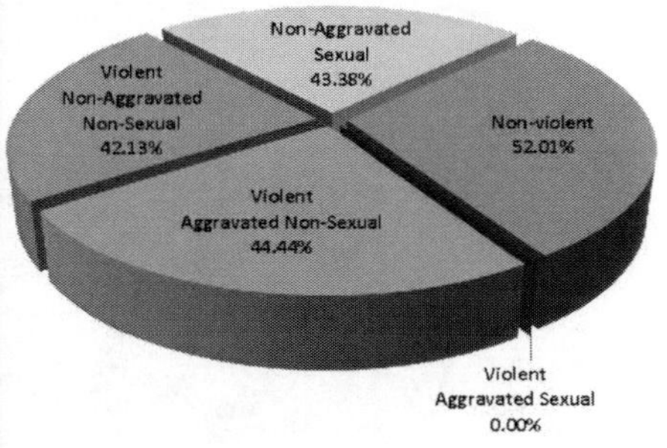

DMS Considerations and Approval Rates History FY 2018 - FY 2022

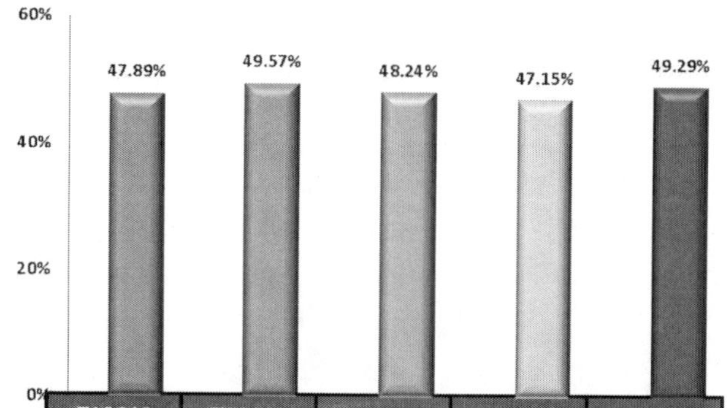

	FY 2018	FY 2019	FY 2020	FY 2021	FY 2022
Cases Considered	19,077	18,947	16,867	14,812	14,073
Cases Approved	9,136	9,392	8,136	6,984	6,936
Approval Rate	47.89%	49.57%	48.24%	47.15%	49.29%

DMS Considerations by Board Members and Parole Commissioners

	TOTAL VOTES	NUMBER APPROVED	APPROVAL RATE	DENIAL RATE
Adams, R.	400	197	49.25%	50.75%
Aiello, R.	330	173	52.42%	47.58%
Brito, E.	1,545	562	36.38%	63.62%
Eck-Massingill, L.	1,984	851	42.89%	57.11%
Evans, I.	1,635	902	55.17%	44.83%
Farley, M.	1,263	626	49.56%	50.44%
Fox, T.	1,882	980	52.07%	47.93%
Gonzalez, R.	1,594	853	53.51%	46.49%
Gutierrez, D.	111	54	48.65%	51.35%
Jernigan, D.	126	58	46.03%	53.97%
Jones, C.	1,169	644	55.09%	44.91%
Kiel, J.	945	532	56.30%	43.70%
LaFavers, J.	1,185	527	44.47%	55.53%
Long, B.	887	476	53.66%	46.34%
Long, T.	1,192	514	43.12%	56.88%
Marton, J.	1,581	602	38.08%	61.92%
Moberley, M.	1,507	886	58.79%	41.21%
Molina, L.	1,595	712	44.64%	55.36%
Ramirez, A.	1,783	859	48.18%	51.82%
Robertson, E.	1,439	782	54.34%	45.66%
Saliagas, W.	954	417	43.71%	56.29%
Speier, C.	1,450	869	59.93%	40.07%
Tejada, R.	2,214	1,013	45.75%	54.25%
Total	**28,771**	**14,089**	**48.97%**	**51.03%**

MEDICALLY RECOMMENDED INTENSIVE SUPERVISION (MRIS)

Medically Recommended Intensive Supervision (MRIS) represents a cooperative effort between the Board, Texas Correctional Office for Offenders with Medical or Mental Impairments (TCOOMMI), Correctional Managed Health Care providers, and TDCJ Parole Division to identify offenders with serious impairments. Provided a release does not constitute a threat to public safety, collaborative decisions are made to release these offenders to a more appropriate environment with supervision.

If an offender qualifies for release to MRIS, the MRIS panel bases its decisions on the offender's medical condition and prognosis, and whether the offender constitutes a threat to public safety.

Offenders must comply with the terms and conditions of the MRIS program and abide by a TCOOMMI-approved release plan. Offenders remain under the care of a physician and in a medically suitable placement.

MRIS Data Comparison Approval by Diagnosis FY 2018 - FY 2022

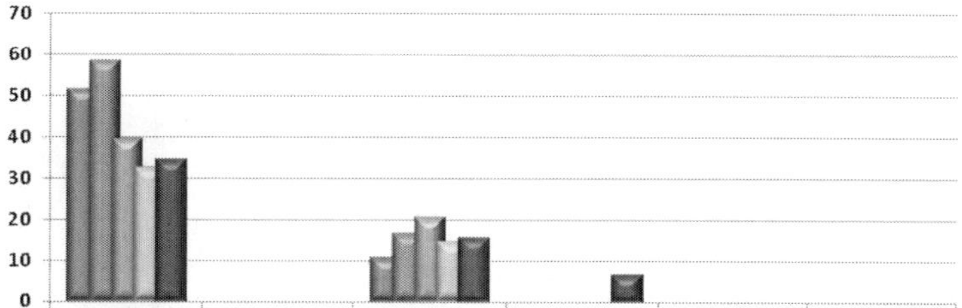

	Terminally Ill	Physically Handicapped	Long Term Care	Elderly	Mentally Ill	Intellectually Disabled
FY 2018	52	0	11	0	0	0
FY 2019	59	0	17	0	0	0
FY 2020	40	0	21	0	0	0
FY 2021	33	0	15	0	0	0
FY 2022	35	0	16	7	0	0

MRIS Considerations and Approval Rates History FY 2018 - FY 2022

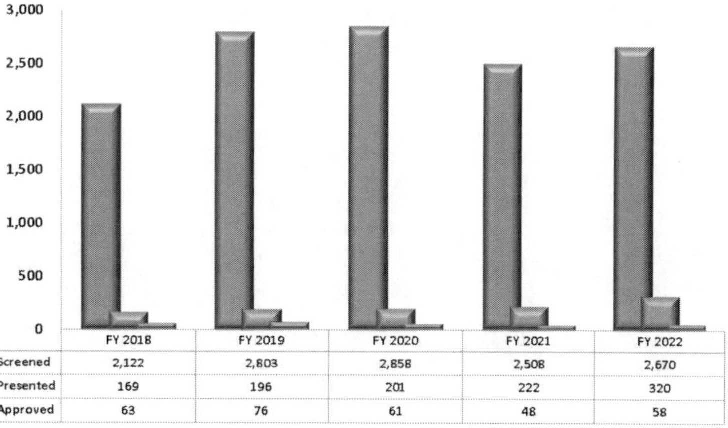

	FY 2018	FY 2019	FY 2020	FY 2021	FY 2022
Screened	2,122	2,803	2,858	2,508	2,670
Presented	169	196	201	222	320
Approved	63	76	61	48	58

(MRIS Data Comparison and Approval Rates by Diagnosis statistics are provided by TCOOMMI.)

SPECIAL REVIEW

Special Review provides a forum for a case to be considered by a Special Review parole panel when it is determined that there is information that was not previously available to the parole panel. If the panel based its decision upon erroneous information or an administrative file processing error, the case may be returned to the original panel to reconsider the decision. Requests for Special Review are considered in the following circumstances:

- A parole panel member who voted with the majority desires to have the decision reconsidered prior to the Next Review (NR) date; or
- A written request on behalf of an offender is received which cites information not previously available to the parole panel; or
- Both parole panel members who voted with the majority are no longer active Board Members or Parole Commissioners and the Presiding Officer places the decision in the Special Review process to be reconsidered prior to the NR date.

In FY 2022, the Board considered a total of 281 Special Review cases. The chart below reflects the disposition of the cases.

Parole Panel Votes after Approval for Special Review

	NUMBER	PERCENT
FI-1 (Parole when Eligible)	90	32.03%
FI-2 (Parole on Specified Date)	20	7.12%
FI-3R (CHANGES)	14	4.98%
FI-4R (SOEP)	2	0.71%
FI-5 (IPTC)	13	4.63%
FI-6 (DWI)	0	0.00%
FI-6R (PRTC, PRSAP)	15	5.34%
FI-7R (SVORI)	0	0.00%
FI-9R (SOTP-9)	6	2.14%
FI-18R (SOTP-18, IFI)	0	0.00%
NR (Set-Off)	71	25.27%
CU/NR Vote	5	1.78%
CU/FI Vote	0	0.00%
CU/SA Vote	1	0.36%
SA (Required to Serve All)	13	4.63%
RMS (Release to Mandatory Supervision)	12	4.27%
DMS (Deny Mandatory Supervision)	19	6.76%
TOTALS	**281**	**100%**

OTHER VOTES AND ACTIVITIES

Transmittals are submitted to parole panels by the Parole Division requesting imposition or withdrawal of special conditions. The total number of transmittal votes was 101,315.

OTHER VOTES	NUMBER
Transmittal Votes	101,315

Board Members and Parole Commissioners conduct victim, offender, attorney, and family interviews via in-person, telephone, or video conference; and educate offenders, victims, and other members of the public regarding the parole process through presentations.

OTHER ACTIVITIES	NUMBER
Office Interviews	1,051
Telephone Interviews	7,644
Correspondence Responses	20,208
Unit Interviews	810
Video Interviews	284
Public Presentations	33
TOTAL	30,030

SUPER INTENSIVE SUPERVISION PROGRAM (SISP)

The Presiding Officer designates regular parole panels and alternate panels. The Super Intensive Supervision Program (SISP) panel considers offenders known to have:

- Committed or threatened to commit an act resulting in a victim; caused bodily injury or serious bodily injury; or placed an individual in danger of bodily injury or serious bodily injury; or
- Had problematic institutional adjustment, such that their accrued good conduct time is not an accurate reflection of their potential for rehabilitation and their release would endanger the public; or identified by TDCJ as a member of an organized prison gang.

Parole Panel Considerations

	PAROLE	MS	TOTALS
Considerations	6,361	1,214	7,575
Imposed	1,045	190	1,235
Percent Imposed	16.43%	15.65%	16.30%

SISP Removal History

	REMOVED	DECEASED	DISCHARGED	REVOKED	OTHER REASON	TOTALS
Parole	717	9	197	68	1	992
MS	58	4	59	33	0	154
TOTALS	775	13	256	101	1	1,146

Revocations for Offenders on SISP

	ALLEGATIONS	
	TOTALS	PERCENT
New Conviction	52	46.43%
Law Violation No New Conviction	4	3.57%
Both Law and Technical Violations	10	8.93%
Technical Only	46	41.07%
Totals	112	100.00%

NOTE: A "Technical Only" violation is a violation of one or more conditions of release, not including the commission of a new offense. "New Offense" includes offenders who have pending felony or misdemeanor charges and possible technical violations at the time of revocation.

INSTITUTIONAL PAROLE ACTIVITY

The Institutional Parole Operations (IPO) performs a variety of functions for the Board. A primary IPO responsibility is interviewing offenders and preparing case summaries for review by a parole panel. The information in the case summary assists the parole panel in making parole or release decisions. In FY 2022, there were 57,924 parole case summaries and 13,478 DMS summaries completed. Additionally, 9 summaries were prepared for clemency reviews on death penalty cases.

Summaries Prepared

	FY 2018	FY 2019	FY 2020	FY 2021	FY 2022
Parole Case Summaries	78,287	76,658	74,538	63,529	57,924
DMS Summaries	18,184	18,452	16,319	14,036	13,478
Clemency Case Summaries	19	18	11	10	9
TOTAL	96,490	95,128	90,868	77,575	71,411

Upon a decision being rendered by a voting panel, the IPO is responsible for notifying the offender of the release decision along with the approval or denial reason(s). In FY 2022, the IPO provided notification via status letters to 61,457 offenders.

Offender Notifications

	FY 2018	FY 2019	FY 2020	FY 2021	FY 2022
Status Letters Provided to Offenders	84,606	83,524	78,681	66,967	61,457

The IPO also provides status information to the family members, victims, and the public concerning offender release decisions. In FY 2022, the IPO responded to 4,806 public phone inquiries and 109,721 offender requests.

HEARING/WAIVER ACTIVITY

Offenders released on supervision are required to comply with both general and any special conditions of release that have been imposed by the Board. In the event an offender is alleged to have violated one or more of the conditions of release, prior to the Board revoking an offender's parole/mandatory supervision, the offender must be afforded an opportunity of a hearing to determine if sufficient evidence exists to show that one or more violations have occurred. An offender may elect to waive such hearing(s) if eligible to do so.

Hearing/Waiver Disposition

Texas Government Code Section 508.282 relates to the time allowed for disposition of alleged violations of parole by a parole panel where the alleged violation occurred. The statutory timeframe from warrant execution of an administrative violation of a release condition to the date of a panel disposition is 41 days. A continuance of a hearing extends the time frame by 15 days.

The offender is entitled to due process in the revocation hearing. These requirements are outlined in Morrissey v. Brewer, 408 U.S. 471, 33L.Ed2d 484, 494 (1972).

There were 16,582 total hearings held in FY 2022, of which 6,887 were subject to statutory timeframes. There were 14,277 total waivers processed in FY 2022, of which 6,397 were subject to statutory timeframes. Cases subject to statutory timeframes where the offender was entitled to a preliminary hearing averaged 23.60 days; those entitled to a revocation hearing averaged 20.90 days; and those entitled to both a preliminary and revocation hearing averaged 32.40.

Hearings and Waivers – Average Processing Time in Days *

	PRELIMINARY	REVOCATION	PRELIMINARY & REVOCATION
AVERAGE	23.60	20.90	32.40

**Start date to parole panel disposition.*

Hearings Conducted by Hearing Officers
FY 2018 – FY 2022

The annual total of hearings illustrates the cumulative workload of the Board's Hearing Officers. In addition to their regular workload, Hearing Officers participate in trainings. Since laws, court decisions, and Board policies change or are reinterpreted over time, the hearing process is constantly changing. The annual training seminar keeps Hearing Officers informed of changes that affect their decision-making responsibilities and the hearing process.

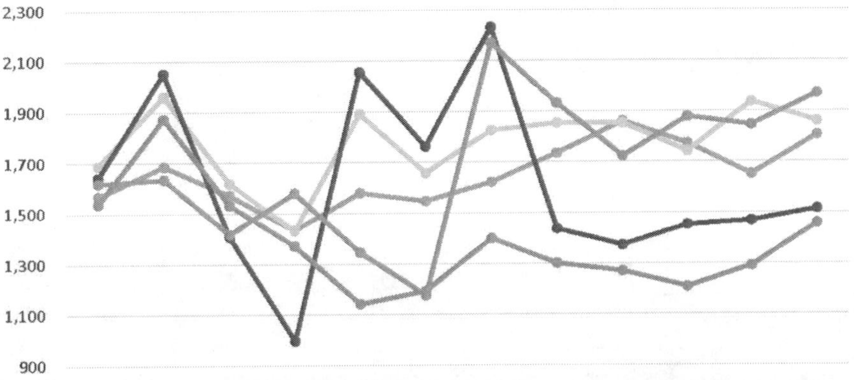

	SEP	OCT	NOV	DEC	JAN	FEB	MAR	APR	MAY	JUN	JUL	AUG	TOTAL
FY 2018	1,569	1,686	1,572	1,433	1,580	1,548	1,622	1,735	1,861	1,773	1,652	1,806	**19,837**
FY 2019	1,689	1,962	1,619	1,432	1,891	1,658	1,826	1,853	1,852	1,742	1,936	1,860	**21,320**
FY 2020	1,642	2,052	1,408	998	2,057	1,762	2,232	1,437	1,372	1,453	1,469	1,515	**19,397**
FY 2021	1,619	1,635	1,418	1,580	1,345	1,176	2,169	1,932	1,722	1,878	1,846	1,969	**20,289**
FY 2022	1,539	1,874	1,533	1,372	1,142	1,193	1,400	1,301	1,270	1,208	1,291	1,459	**16,582**

Hearings Conducted by Hearing Officers
FY 2018 – FY 2022

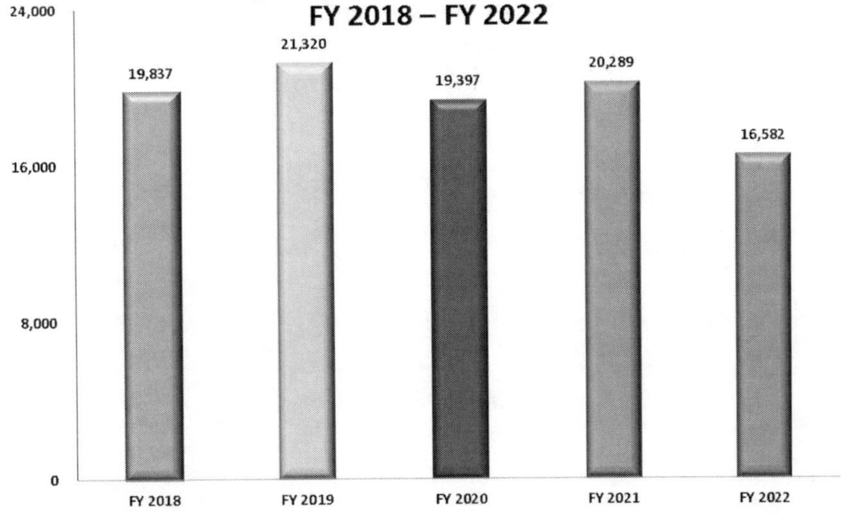

Allegations Presented for Administrative Decisions

By Allegation (Hearings and Waivers)

	NUMBER
New Conviction	7,471
Law Violation No New Conviction	1,340
Both Law and Technical Violations	3,320
Technical Only	13,534
Erroneous Release	0
TOTAL	25,665

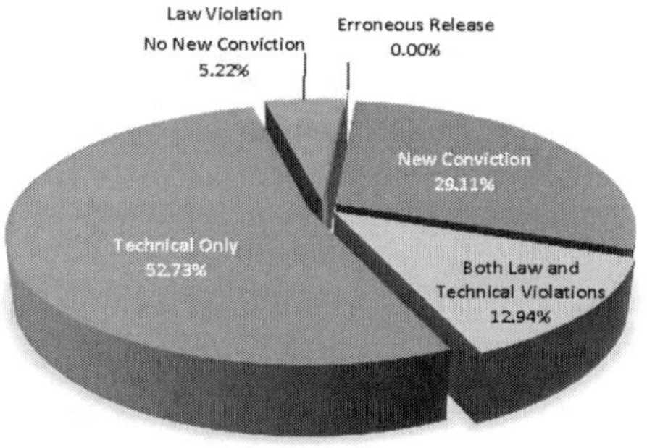

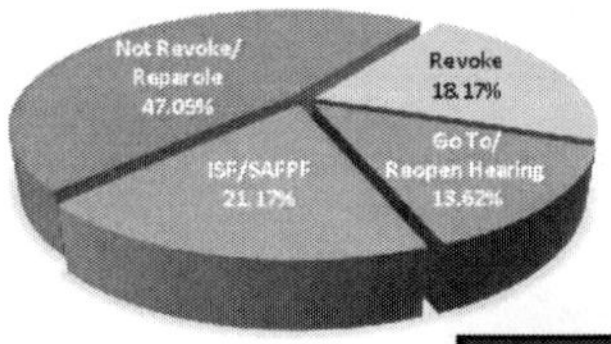

By Decision

	NON-REVOCATION				GO TO HEARING	REOPEN HEARING	PLACE IN NORMAL REVIEW	REVOKE	TOTAL ACTIONS
	CONTINUE SUPERVISION	TRANSFER TO ISF FACILITY	REPAROLE	SAFPF					
FY 2018	11,805	8,278	1	849	10,574	37	3	6,179	37,726
	31.29%	21.94%	0.00%	2.25%	28.03%	0.10%	0.01%	16.38%	
FY 2019	14,444	7,537	0	753	10,824	54	4	5,397	39,013
	37.02%	19.32%	0.00%	1.93%	27.74%	0.14%	0.01%	13.83%	
FY 2020	13,615	6,569	0	558	10,760	72	0	4,092	35,666
	38.17%	18.42%	0.00%	1.56%	30.17%	0.20%	0.00%	11.47%	
FY 2021	13,159	5,255	0	289	11,145	23	0	3,639	33,510
	39.27%	15.68%	0.00%	0.86%	33.26%	0.07%	0.00%	10.86%	
FY 2022	12,075	5,198	0	234	3,462	33	0	4,663	25,665
	47.05%	20.25%	0.00%	0.91%	13.49%	0.13%	0.00%	18.17%	

Revocations Compared to Hearings and Waivers FY 2013 – FY 2022

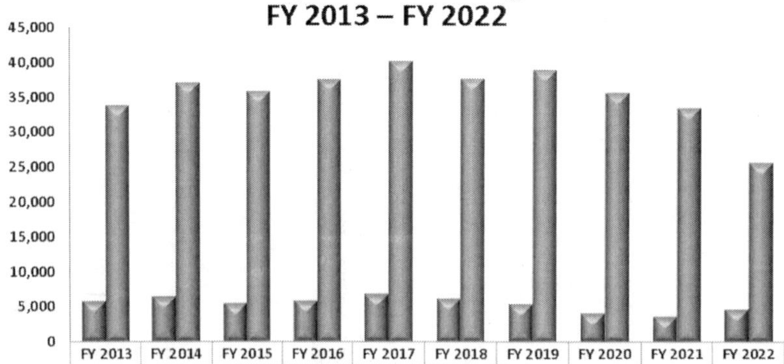

	FY 2013	FY 2014	FY 2015	FY 2016	FY 2017	FY 2018	FY 2019	FY 2020	FY 2021	FY 2022
Revoke	5,850	6,455	5,501	5,895	6,830	6,179	5,397	4,092	3,639	4,663
Total	33,816	37,134	35,853	37,618	40,321	37,726	39,013	35,666	33,510	25,665

Administrative Decisions by Board Members and Parole Commissioners

	NON-REVOCATION				GO TO HEARING	REOPEN HEARING	PLACE IN NORMAL REVIEW	REVOKE	TOTAL ACTIONS
	CONTINUE SUPERVISION	TRANSFER TO ISF FACILITY	SAFPF	REPAROLE					
Adams, M.	306	150	2	0	0	1	0	131	**590**
Aiello, R.	252	113	3	0	0	0	0	95	**463**
Brito, E.	1,412	875	39	0	2	9	0	620	**2,957**
Eck-Massingill, L.	1,974	740	42	0	4	2	0	443	**3,205**
Evans, I.	1,224	415	27	0	3	2	0	493	**2,164**
Farley, M.	1,122	473	14	0	3	0	0	410	**2,022**
Fox, T.	1,702	691	35	0	1	3	0	637	**3,069**
Gonzalez, R.	1,184	421	29	0	4	3	0	471	**2,112**
Gutierrez, D.	69	75	6	0	0	0	0	41	**191**
Jernigan, D.	204	73	0	0	1	0	0	57	**335**
Jones, C.	970	409	13	0	2	2	0	352	**1,748**
Kiel, J.	1,059	266	8	0	12	5	0	374	**1,724**
LaFavers, J.	1,046	662	31	0	2	2	0	517	**2,260**
Long, B.	1,075	285	11	0	12	8	0	379	**1,770**
Long, T.	1,088	498	13	0	5	3	0	375	**1,982**
Marton, J.	1,524	922	38	0	2	11	0	662	**3,159**
Moberley, M.	1,356	516	29	0	3	3	0	374	**2,281**
Molina, L.	683	407	21	0	2	3	0	542	**1,658**
Ramirez, A.	709	445	27	0	1	1	0	611	**1,794**
Robertson, E.	1,457	623	25	0	2	0	0	531	**2,638**
Saliagas, W.	1,087	274	8	0	10	3	0	406	**1,788**
Speier, C.	688	390	21	0	1	3	0	435	**1,538**
Tejada, R.	2,215	772	34	0	4	3	0	527	**3,555**
TOTALS	24,406	10,495	476	0	76	67	0	9,483	45,003

Parole Panels have various options in the revocation process such as sending the offender to an Intermediate Sanction Facility (ISF) or Substance Abuse Felony Punishment Facility (SAFPF).

Decisions to Send Offender to ISF or SAFPF

	NUMBER OF CASES	PERCENT
New Conviction	901	16.59%
Law Violation No New Conviction	7	0.13%
Both Law and Technical Violations	96	1.77%
Technical Only	4,428	81.52%
TOTALS	5,432	100.00%

Disposition to ISF/SAFPF

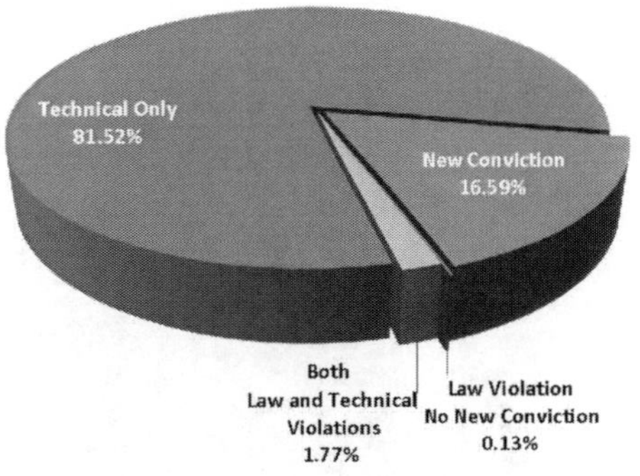

The parole panel that reviews a revocation case decides whether the offender will continue on supervision, with or without modification of conditions of release. In the case of Erroneous Release, the panel can recommend that the offender be placed in the normal parole review process upon return to TDCJ CID, parole if eligible (FI-1), or continue on the existing release certificate.

Decisions to Continue Supervision or Reparole

	CASES	PERCENT
New Conviction	2,181	18.06%
Law Violation No New Conviction	523	4.33%
Both Law and Technical Violations	1,318	10.92%
Technical Only	8,053	66.69%
Erroneous Release	0	0.00%
TOTALS	12,075	100.00%

Decisions to Revoke or Place in Normal Review

	CASES	PERCENT
New Conviction	3,200	68.63%
Law Violation No New Conviction	96	2.06%
Both Law and Technical Violations	332	7.12%
Technical Only	1,035	22.20%
Erroneous Release	0	0.00%
TOTALS	4,663	100.00%

Disposition to Continue Supervision or Reparole

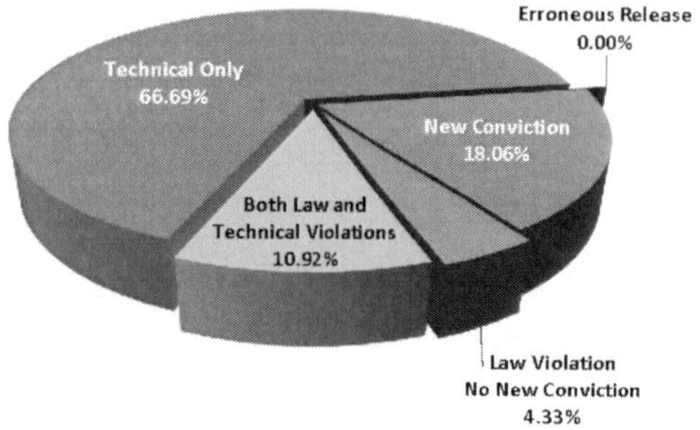

Disposition to Revoke or Place in Normal Review

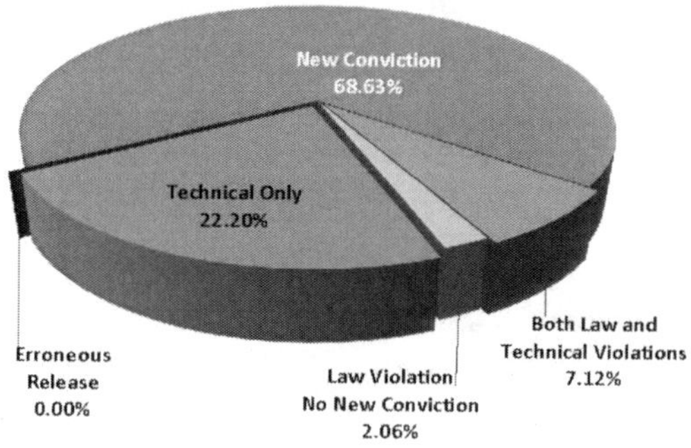

History of Offenders Revoked by Grounds for Revocation FY 2018 - FY 2022

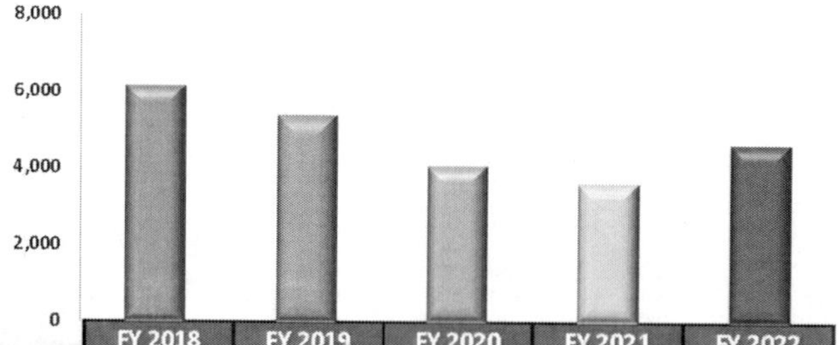

	FY 2018	FY 2019	FY 2020	FY 2021	FY 2022
New Conviction	4,783	4,404	3,480	3,085	3,200
Law Violation No New Conviction	39	53	13	46	96
Both Law and Technical Violations	252	176	72	137	332
Technical Only	1,105	764	527	371	1,035
TOTALS	6,179	5,397	4,092	3,639	4,663

Revocations by Release Type
Parole/Mandatory Supervision
Monthly Totals

	SEP	OCT	NOV	DEC	JAN	FEB	MAR	APR	MAY	JUN	JUL	AUG	TOTAL
Parole	265	347	329	318	258	235	367	288	279	306	235	242	**3,469**
MS	3	6	7	2	3	3	2	6	3	8	3	4	**50**
DMS	86	109	98	104	91	101	109	93	90	94	85	84	**1,144**
TOTALS	354	462	434	424	352	339	478	387	372	408	323	330	**4,663**

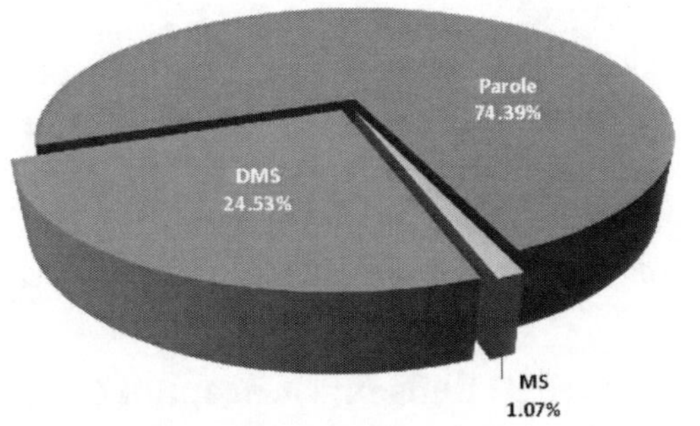

Decisions
(Waivers/Hearings Processed)

	PREL	REV ONLY	PREL & REV SIMULTANEOUSLY	TRANSMITTALS	TOTALS
Total Waivers Processed *	3,427	10,754	96	N/A	**14,277**
Total Hearings Processed **	6,745	10,748	N/A	N/A	**17,493**
Transmittals ***	N/A	N/A	N/A	512	**512**
TOTAL WAIVERS/ HEARINGS/TRANSMITTALS	**10,172**	**21,502**	**96**	**512**	**32,282**

** 6,397 Waivers were subject to statutory timeframes.*
*** 6,887 Hearings were subject to statutory timeframes.*
**** Cases transmitted to a parole panel for reconsideration subsequent to a decision resulting from a hearing or waiver.*

EXECUTIVE CLEMENCY

The authority for the Governor to grant executive clemency is in Article 4, Section 11, of the Texas Constitution. In all criminal cases, except treason and impeachment, the Governor may grant clemency upon written recommendation of a majority of the Board after a conviction or successful completion of a term of deferred adjudication community supervision. The Constitution authorizes the Governor to grant pardons, reprieves, and commutations of sentence. The Board, pursuant to Section 508.036(b)(1), Government Code, adopted rules governing the clemency process for noncapital and capital cases.

Clemency Process

The process begins when an individual or their representative submits an application along with the appropriate documents. The process includes notification of the trial officials identified in Section 508.115, Government Code, and the victim, if one is identified.

Clemency Decision

The Governor makes the final decision to grant clemency. The Board may only recommend or not recommend that the Governor grant clemency.

Board Actions on Noncapital Cases

In noncapital cases, the Board considers applications for full pardons and restoration of rights of citizenship, pardons for innocence, conditional pardons, reprieves, commutations of sentence, remissions of fines and forfeitures, restoration of firearm rights and civil rights of a federal or military offense, and restoration of driver's licenses. In FY 2022, the Board considered 66 noncapital cases (see table below).

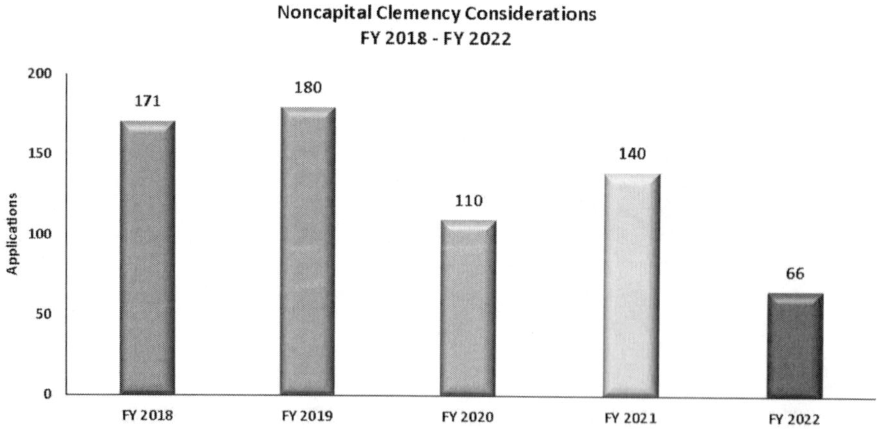

In FY 2022, the Board recommended that the Governor grant 26 noncapital clemency requests out of 66 applications considered, or 39% of the applications considered (see table below).

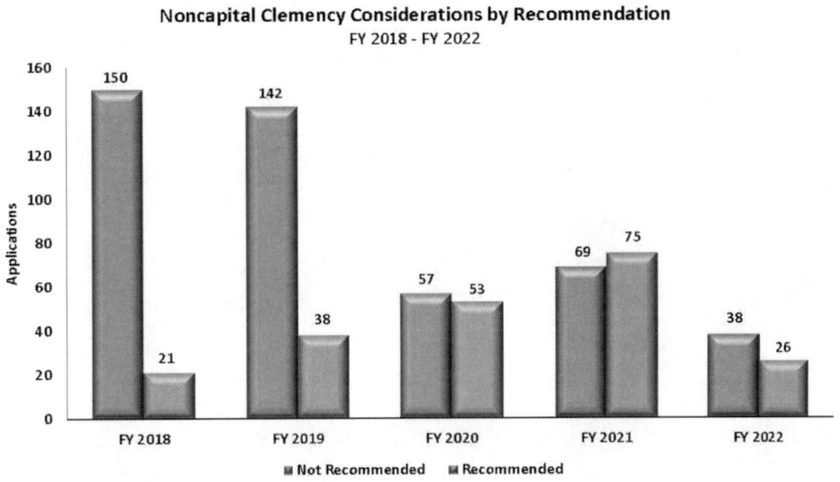

NOTE: The number of cases considered may differ from the number of cases voted when cases are referred to the Board for consideration during one fiscal year and voted on during the following fiscal year.

Board Actions on Capital Cases

In capital cases, the Board considers applications for commutation of death sentence to lesser penalty and a reprieve of execution. Upon request, the Board may conduct an interview with the offender. The Governor may also grant a one-time 30-day reprieve of execution without a recommendation from the Board. In FY 2022, six applications were received which requested a commutation of sentence. Of the six applications, five also included a request for a reprieve. Five of the applicants received stays of execution prior to consideration by the Board. In FY 2022, the Board conducted two interviews, considered four applications for clemency, and did not recommend clemency (see table below).

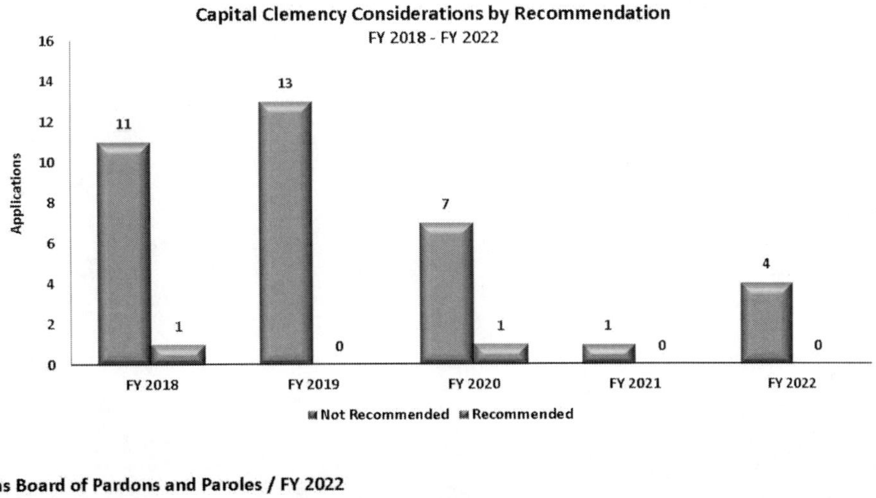

AGENCY EXPENDITURES

FY 2022 BUDGET

FY 2022 Budget Total	$ 30,853,763
Hearing Operations	$ 7,933,633
Institutional Operations	$ 14,787,698
Board Operations	$ 6,400,759
Clemency	$ 762,272
Capital: Vehicle	$ 263,513
Capital: Information Technology	$ 105,306
Victim Liaison Grant	$ 343,548
Violence Against Women Grant	$ 257,034

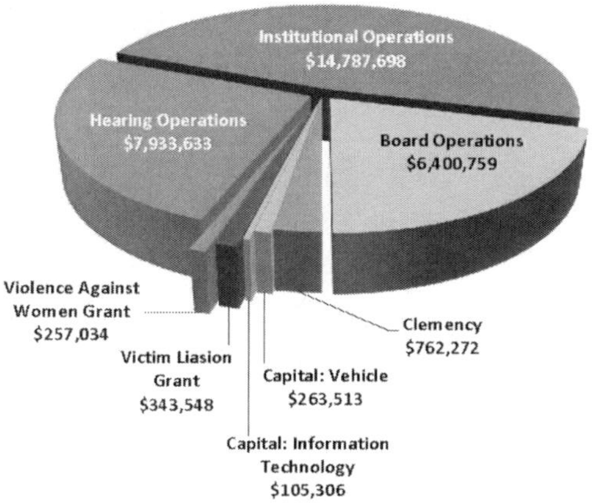

FY 2022 EXPENDITURES (ACTUAL)

FY 2022 Expenditure Total	$ 26,992,035
Hearing Operations	$ 6,893,170
Institutional Operations	$ 12,994,255
Board Operations	$ 5,758,492
Clemency	$ 731,669
Capital: Vehicle	$ 186,018
Capital: Information Technology	$ 93,740
Victim Liaison Grant	$ 254,066
Violence Against Women Grant	$ 80,625

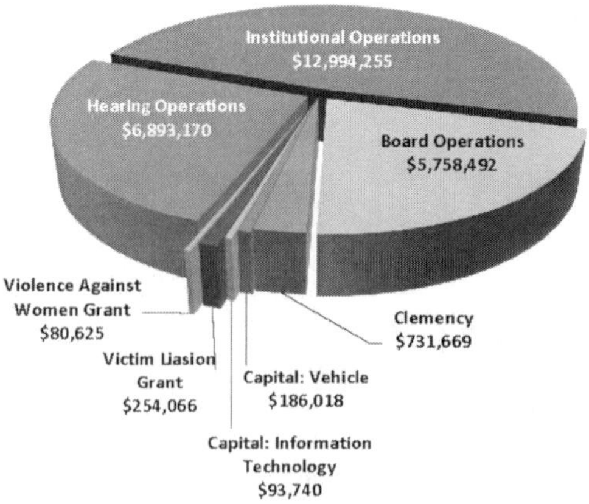

NOTE: Board Operations includes expenditure and budget received from the Victim Liaison Grant and the Domestic Violence and Human Trafficking Restorative Justice Program Grant.

Risk Assessment Worksheet

Static Factors

Question	Select One	Your Score
The Commitment Offense: Does the commitment offense include an UUMV, Burglary Of A Habitation, Burglary of a Motor Vehicle, or Forgery charge?	No = 0 Points Yes = 1 Point	
History of Supervisory release Revocations for felony offenses: Is there a history of supervisory release revocations for felony offenses?	No probation, parole or mandatory supervision revocations = 0 Points One Revocation = 1 Point More than one revocation = 3 Points	
Prior Incarcerations: Does the offender have prior incarcerations?	None = 0 Points One or two prior incarcerations = 1 Point Three or more prior incarcerations = 3 Points	
Employment History: Does the offender's employment history include six months of continuous full-time employment or school attendance in the two years before incarceration?	Yes = 0 Points No - 1 Point	
Age at first admission: What was the offender's age at first admission to a juvenile or adult correctional facility?	26 or older = 0 Points 18 to 25 = 1 Point 17 or Under = 2 Points	
Total Static Points		

To complete the Risk Assessment Static Factors, read the question in column one, look at the number next to the answer in column two, and write that number down in column three.

Once all five questions have been answered, add the numbers in column three and write the total down at the bottom. This number is the Total Static Points.

Dynamic Factors

Question	Select One	Your Score
What is the Offender's Current Age?	Under 25 years old = 3 Points 25-34 years old = 2 Points 35-44 years old = 1 Point Over 45 = 0 Points	
Is the offender a confirmed member of a security threat group (Gang)?	Active STG (Gang) Member = 1 Points No Gang "Tag" = 0 Points	
Were there any educational, vocational, or certified on-the-job training programs completed during the present incarceration?	Yes = 0 Points No = 1 Points	
Is there any prison disciplinary conduct in the last eighteen months?	None = 0 Points Demoted below entry level OR good time lost = 1 Point Zero balance of good time = 2 Points	
What is the offender's current prison custody level?	Minimum Out (outside trusty S-2) = 0 Points Minimum In (inside trusty S-3) = 1 Point	

	Medium, close custody or Ad. Seg. = 2 Points	
Total Dynamic Points		

To complete the Risk Assessment Dynamic Factors, read the question in column one, look at the number next to the answer in column two, and write that number down in column three.

Once all five questions have been answered, add the numbers in column three and write the total down at the bottom. This number is the Total Dynamic Points.

Total Risk Assessment Points

Total Static Points	
Total Dynamic Points	
Your Total Points	

Enter the Total Static and Dynamic points on the Total Risk Assessment Points worksheet. Add the numbers together to get "Your Total Points" or the Total Risk Assessment Factor Points.

Next, Look at the chart below. Locate the block that contains the number range of Total Risk Assessment Factor Points in the column with the correct gender. Once that is found, looked in the first column and find the Assigned Risk Level on the row with the correct number of points.

For example, if the Total Risk Assessment Factor Points was 11 for a male, then the Assigned Risk Level is "High Risk".

Score Assigned Risk Level

Assigned Risk Level	Male (Total Points)	Female (Total Points)
Low Risk	3 or less	3 or less
Moderate Risk	4-8	4-9
High Risk	9-15	10+
Highest Risk	16+	N/A

Offense Severity Class

Every felony offense in the Texas Penal Code has been assigned an Offense Severity Rating, which the Board is required to periodically review. The Offense Severity Classes range from Low (for non-violent crimes) to Highest (for capital murder), with the most serious active offense providing the rating in the event there are multiple concurrent offenses.

Look at the chart in Appendix 2 to determine your Offense Severity Level and enter it below.

Offense Severity Level	

Parole Guideline Score

The two components of the guidelines, Risk Assessment and Offense Severity, are merged into a matrix that creates the offender's Parole Guideline Score. There are separate risk scales for male and female offenders.

Parole Guidelines Scores range from one, for an individual with the poorest probability for success, to seven, for an offender with the greatest probability of success while on parole.

The guidelines are neither automatic nor presumptive of whether an offender will receive parole. Parole panel members retain the discretion to vote outside the guidelines when circumstances of an individual case merit doing so.

After determining both the Offense Severity Level and the Total Risk Assessment Factor Points, these two components are then merged to determine the Parole Guideline Score (PGS).

The PGS is determined by locating the intersection of the total number of Risk Assessment Factor Points from the Risk Assessment worksheet and the Offense Severity Level ranking.

Look at the charts below. Locate on the chart that corresponds to the inmates gender. Look at the top row of the chart and locate the column that contains the number of the Total Risk Assessment Factor points calculated earlier. Now follow that column down until you reach the row that contains the Offense Severity Ranking Level found in the column on the left. The number where the Total Risk Assessment Factor Points and the Offense Severity Ranking Level intersect is the Parole Guideline Score.

As an example, a Risk Assessment Factor Point of 2 with a Moderate Offense Severity Level for a male would result in a Parole Guideline Level of 6, as indicated in the 4th box down in the far right column of the chart below.

Risk Levels for Males

Offense Severity Class	16 Risk Factor Points Highest **H+**	9-15 Risk Factor Points High **H**	4-8 Risk Factor Points Moderate **M**	0-3 Risk Factor Points Low **L**
Highest **H+**	Parole Guideline Score: **1**	Parole Guideline Score: **2**	Parole Guideline Score: **2**	Parole Guideline Score: **3**
High **H**	Parole Guideline Score: **2**	Parole Guideline Score: **3**	Parole Guideline Score: **4**	Parole Guideline Score: **4**
Moderate **M**	Parole Guideline Score: **2**	Parole Guideline Score: 3	Parole Guideline Score: **5**	Parole Guideline Score: **6**
Low **L**	Parole Guideline Score: **3**	Parole Guideline Score: **4**	Parole Guideline Score: **6**	Parole Guideline Score: **7**

Risk Levels for Females

Offense Severity Class	Risk Level: Highest (10+)	Risk Level: Moderate (4-9)	Risk Level: Low (3 or less)
Highest H+	Parole Guideline Score: 2	Parole Guideline Score: 2	Parole Guideline Score: 3
High H	Parole Guideline Score: 3	Parole Guideline Score: 4	Parole Guideline Score: 4
Moderate M	Parole Guideline Score: 3	Parole Guideline Score: 5	Parole Guideline Score: 6
Low L	Parole Guideline Score: 4	Parole Guideline Score: 6	Parole Guideline Score: 7

One of the charts in the next section provides the most recent statistics for the approval rates for parole for each Guideline Score.

Other Factors That Influence the Parole Board

Not every aspect of an offender's case is measured by the parole guidelines. Board members and parole commissioners also consider other factors , such as 1) the original offense, 2) sentence length, 3) behavior since incarceration, 4) programs completed, and 5) support systems strength and parole plans.

During a parole review, voters consider:

The original crime or crimes an individual committed.;
Offender's criminal history;
Drug and alcohol involvement;
Conduct in prison;
Life before prison;
Victim statements;
Protests from trial officials;
Completion of prison programs;
The post-prison parole plan;
Parole support letters;
Parole package.

Parole Voting Options

Now that the voting members have calculate the offender's Parole Guideline Score, they have several options on voting. Other than a **Serve-All** (offender serves all remaining time) or a **Set Off** (parole not granted - offender is reviewed in 6 months to 10 years), the members of the Board have several options.

A parole panel consists of three parole panel members. The members for each area are listed in Appendix 3. The first voting member will review the file and cast a vote. The file will move to the second voting member to cast a vote. If both votes are the same the parole file is completed. If the first two votes are different then the parole file will move to the third panel member for a vote to break the tie. There must be a majority of two votes to become final.

Approval Votes

FI-1 Release offender on parole supervision when eligible.

FI-2 Release on parole on a specified future date.

FI-3R Transfer to a TDCJ rehabilitation program, such as Changes/Life skills, Voyager, or Segovia Pre-Release Center no earlier than a specified date at least three months with release on parole after completion. Release to parole only after completion of the program.

F1-4R Transfer to a Sex Offender Education Program (SOEP) no earlier than a specified date for at least four months from specified date.

FI-5 Transfer to an In-Prison Therapeutic Community Program (IPTC), with release to an aftercare component after completion of the program.

FI-6 Transfer to DWI rehabilitation program with release to continuum of care program.

FI-6R Transfer to a rehabilitation program, such as the Pre-Release Therapeutic Community (PRTC) or Pre-Release Substance Abuse Program (PRSAP), no earlier than specified date for at least six months with release on parole after completion.

FI-7R Transfer to Serious and Violent Offender Reentry Initiative (SVORI), then released to parole only after program completion and no earlier than specified date for at least seven months.

FI-9R Transfer to the Sex Offender Treatment Program (SOTP-9) no earlier than specified date for at least nine months, with release on parole after completion but not earlier than nine months from specified date.

FI-18R Transfer to the Sex Offender Treatment Program (SOTP-18) or the InnerChange Freedom Initiative (IFI) no earlier than specified date for at least 18 months, with release on parole after completion.

CU-FI Designates the date an offender serving consecutive sentences would have been eligible for parole if single sentence.

RMS Release to mandatory supervision

Denial Votes

NR (Next Review): Deny parole and set time for next parole consideration. State law requires annual reviews except for certain violent or sexual cases.

SA (Serve All): Deny parole with no regular subsequent review, requiring offender to serve the balance of their sentence if the discharge date occurs in less than three years.

CU-NR Deny favorable action and set next review in consecutive sentence case.

CU-SA Require offender to serve all of current sentence in consecutive sentence case.

DMS Denies Mandatory Supervision (and sets next review date) because offender's accrued good conduct time does not accurately reflect potential for rehabilitation and offender's release would endanger the public.

SB 45 Cases Which Requires A Full Board Vote

SB 45 cases involve capital felons who are eligible for parole, persons convicted of an offense under Section 20A.03 [Continuous Trafficking of Persons], Section 21.02 [Continuous Sexual Abuse of Young Child or Children], Section 21.11(a)(1) [Indecency with a Child], or Section 22.021 [Aggravated

Sexual Assault] of the Penal Code or offenders that are required to serve at least 35 calendar years before becoming eligible for parole have more limited set of voting options as stated in Senate Bill 45 of the 74th Legislature. These cases require two-thirds majority vote of the full Board for parole approval.

SB 45 cases are eligible for up to a five year set-off. This means the offender's next parole eligibility date could be up to five years in the future.

SB 45 Voting Options

FI-1 Release when eligible with conditions (if any).

F1-4R Transfer to a TDCJ Sex Offender Education Program (SOEP). Release to parole only after program completion and not earlier than four months from a specified date.

FI-9R Transfer to an TDCJ Sex Offender Treatment Program (SOTP-9) then released to parole only after program completion and not earlier than nine months from specified date.

FI-18R Transfer to an TDCJ rehabilitation treatment program. Release to parole only after program competition and no earlier than eighteen months from the specified date. TDCJ programs may include Sex Offender Treatment Program (SOTP-18), or the InnerChange Freedom Initiative (IFI). The specified date cannot be more than three years from the current panel decision date.

Denial Votes:

NR (Next Review): Deny release and set the next review date for 36 or 60 months following the panel decision date.

SA (Serve All): Deny parole with no regular subsequent review, in the event the offender's minimum or maximum expiration date is less than 60 months away.

HB 1914 Cases Which Requires A Full Board Vote

HB 1914 cases involve capital felons who are eligible for parole, persons convicted of an offense under Section 20A.03 [Continuous Trafficking of Persons], Section 21.02 [Continuous Sexual Abuse of Young Child or Children], Section 21.11(a)(1) [Indecency with a Child], or Section 22.021 [Aggravated Sexual Assault] of the Penal Code, or persons required under Texas

Government Code Section 508.145(c) to serve 35 calendar years before becoming eligible for release on parole. These cases have a limited set of voting options require two-thirds majority vote of the full Board for parole approval.

HB 1914 cases are eligible for up to a ten year set-off. This means the offender's next parole eligibility date could be up to ten years in the future.

HB 1914 Voting Options

FI-1 Release when eligible with conditions (if any).

F1-4R Transfer to a TDCJ Sex Offender Education Program (SOEP). Release to parole only after program completion and not earlier than four months from a specified date.

FI-9R Transfer to an TDCJ Sex Offender Treatment Program (SOTP-9) then released to parole only after program completion and not earlier than nine months from specified date.

FI-18R Transfer to an TDCJ rehabilitation treatment program. Release to parole only after program competition and no earlier than eighteen months from the specified date. TDCJ programs may include Sex Offender Treatment Program (SOTP-18), or the InnerChange Freedom Initiative (IFI). The specified date cannot be more than three years from the current panel decision date.

Denial Votes:

NR (Next Review): Deny release and set the next review date for 36, 60, 84, or 120 months following the panel decision date.

SA (Serve All): Deny parole with no regular subsequent review in the event the offender's minimum or maximum expiration date is less than 120 months away. The offender will continue to serve their sentence until that date.

* **NOTE** * The main difference between SB 45 and HB 1914 is SB 45 convicted offenders can get a set-off of up to 5 years and HB 1914 convicted offenders can get a set-off of up to 10 years.

HB 1433 Cases - Discretionary Mandatory Supervision Voting Options

This legislation requires the Board to review some offenders prior to release to mandatory supervision. To deny mandatory supervision, a parole panel must determine that accrued good conduct time is not an accurate reflection of the offender's potential for rehabilitation AND that the offender's release would endanger the public.

HB 1433 only applies to an offender eligible for release to mandatory supervision if the sentence is for an offense committed on or after September 1, 1996.

The two voting options are:

DMS Deny release to mandatory supervision and set the next mandatory supervision review date one year from the panel decision date. The vote is either D-1 or D-2 to deny DMS.

- D-1 - The record indicates the inmate accrued good conduct time is not an accurate reflection of the inmates potential for rehabilitation
- D-2 The record indicates that the inmate's release would endanger the public.

RMS Release to mandatory supervision.

Rule 145.13 Cases - Voting Options

This voting option is designed for offenders with consecutive sentences if each of the offenses committed were on or after September 1, 1987.

CU/FI Designate the date on which the offender would have been eligible for release on parole if the offender had been sentenced to serve a single sentence. This date shall be within a three-year incarceration period following the panel decision

CU/NU Deny favorable parole action and set the next review date at one year from the panel decision date. If the offender is serving an offense under Section 508.149(a), Government Code, or second or third degree under Section 22.04, Penal Code; the next review date (month/year) may be set at any date in the five-year incarceration period following the panel decision date, but in no event shall it be less than one calendar year from the panel decision date.

CU/SA- If the offender is serving an offense under Section 508.149(a), Government Code, or second or third degree under Section 22.04, Penal Code; deny release and order serve-all, but in no event shall this be utilized if the offender's maximum expiration date is over five years from the date of the panel decision. If the offender is not serving an offense under Section 508.149(a),

Government Code, deny release and order serve-all, but in no event shall this be utilized if the offender's maximum expiration date is over one year from the date of the panel decision.

MRIS Voting Options

Medically Recommended Intensive Supervision (MRIS) Program is for offenders who are mentally ill, mentally retarded, elderly, terminally ill, physically handicapped, or require long-term care are considered for release by a parole panel. The panel, based on the offender's condition and medical evaluation, may release an offender who does not constitute a threat to public safety or a threat to commit an offense.

A special MRIS panel determines the discretionary release of MRIS identified offenders. The two voting options are:

FI-1 Approve MRIS and impose Special Condition "0" which specifies the offender shall comply with the terms and conditions of MRIS Program and abide by the approved release plan. The offender will remain under the care of a physician and in a medically suitable place while under Special Condition "0".

Deny Deny MRIS release.

Special Conditions Attached to Parole

Texas Board of Pardons and Paroles (Board) determine conditions of parole and mandatory supervision. Special conditions are conditions imposed in addition to the standard conditions of parole or mandatory supervision. Unless otherwise provided, any condition may be imposed before or after release and shall remain in effect until specifically removed by a parole panel.

Condition	Name	Description
O.01	Residence During Release	Unless otherwise provided, the offender shall reside in the county where he resided at the time he committed the offense for which he was sentenced to the Correction Institutions Division (CID), or the county of the offense for which the offender was sentenced to the CID, if the offender was not a resident of the State of Texas. This condition appears on almost all parolees.
O.03	Controlled Substance Testing	This condition appears for the release of all offenders. It is the random drug testing while under supervision.
O.04	Post Secondary Education Reimbursement (PSER)	This condition appears for the release of all offenders who enroll in such courses at a TDCJ facility on or after 09/01/1995. It is the reimbursement for post-secondary education programs.
O.05	Substance Abuse Treatment	This condition shall be imposed immediately before release after completion of the In-Prison Therapeutic Community (IPTC) program, established under Section 501.0931 of the Texas Government Code, to ensure participation in a drug and alcohol continuum of care treatment program, post release.
O.06	Child Safety Zone	This condition shall be imposed for offenders whose victim was a child younger than seventeen (17) years of age and are serving a sentence for any of the following listed offenses and/or Texas Penal Codes: • 20.04(a)(4) Aggravated Kidnapping with intent to inflict bodily injury or violate or abuse sexually • 21.02

		Continuous Sexual Abuse of Young Child or Children • 21.11 Indecency with a Child • 22.011 Sexual Assault (formerly Rape) • 22.021 Aggravated Sexual Assault • 25.02 Prohibited Sexual Conduct (formerly Incest) 08/15/17 PD/POP-2.2.25 Page 4 of 11 • 43.25 Sexual Performance by a Child • 43.26 Possession or Promotion of Child Pornography • 30.02(d) Burglary of a Habitation with intent to commit a violation of an offense listed above
O.07	Community Service for Certain Releasees	This condition shall be imposed for offenders serving a sentence for certain crimes committed because of bias or prejudice. With this condition, offenders are required to perform not less than 300 hours of community service at projects that serve the persons or groups who were the targets of the offender. This condition requires an affirmative finding by the sentencing court under Article 42.014 of the Texas Code of Criminal Procedure. The affirmative finding must be noted on the Judgment and Sentence. Those offenses are listed under the following Texas Penal Code: • 28.02 Arson • 28.03 Criminal Mischief • 28.08 Graffiti
C	Prohibited Financial Activities	This condition prohibits certain financial activities by offenders who have been convicted of theft or fraud or who have an established propensity for engaging in theft or fraudulent criminal behavior. At any time Special Condition "C" is in effect the offender shall: - Not open or maintain more than one checking account; - Not open or maintain more than one savings account; - Not obtain or maintain more than one credit or debit card; and - Not participate in electronic financial transmissions without prior written approval of the

		offender's supervising parole officer
D	Release to Detainer	Release the offender to a detainer for deportation or transfer to Immigration and Customs Enforcement (ICE) or another law enforcement or correctional agency.
E	Educational Skill Level	This condition shall be imposed for mentally competent offenders who have not attained a 6th grade education level prior to release. The parolee must participate in education or vocational programs. This can include ESL, literacy classes, adult basic education classes, vocational training, or other appropriate training as instructed by the supervising parole officer.
I	Employer Notification	Special Condition "I" is intended to inform any prospective employer of an offender's criminal history if the offender will be employed in a position of financial responsibility.
ISF	Intermediate Sanction Facility	A special condition imposed by a parole panel that will serve to punish, rehabilitate, or reform an offender in response to a violation of a condition of release to parole or mandatory supervision following a hearing or proceeding concerning alleged violations under Chapter 146 of the Board Rules.
L	Maximum Level of Supervision	A higher level of supervision is needed upon release or after violations of parole or mandatory supervision.
M	Sex Offender Registration & DNA Submission	Sex offender registration and the submission of DNA is required as a condition of parole or mandatory supervision.
N	Prohibition on Internet Access	At any time Special Condition "N" is in effect, the offender is prohibited from using the internet or any type of electronic device used for internet access.
No Contact	No Contact	At any time this condition is in effect, the offender can have no contact for a child or children of a legally recognized parent or spouse.
P	Special Needs	At any time Special Condition "P" is in effect, the

		offender shall participate in mental health assessments and evaluation, Intellectual Developmental Disorder assessment and evaluations, mental health/intellectual development disorder treatment or counseling, rehabilitation training, and use medication as prescribed.
R	Restitution	Payment by the offender to the victim of the offense through the Division for financial loss sustained as a result of the offense.
S	Substance Abuse	At any time this condition is in effect, unless modified or withdrawn by a parole panel, an offender shall not unlawfully use drugs, narcotics, or controlled substances or use intoxicating inhalants, or consume alcoholic beverages. The parolee will submit to urinalysis monitoring, not enter an establishment where the primary function is the sale and dispensing of alcoholic beverages, and obey all driving restrictions. Some offenders will be required to attend substance abuse treatment programs or counseling.
SAFP	Substance Abuse Felony Program	A special condition imposed by a parole panel that will serve to confine and treat an offender and requires the offender to participate in a post-release drug or alcohol abuse continuum of care treatment plan. The special condition may be imposed when a parole panel renders a finding following a hearing or proceeding concerning alleged violations of the terms and conditions of parole or mandatory supervision under Chapter 146 of the Board Rules for an offender who is a suitable candidate as determined by the suitability criteria.
SISP	Super Intensive Supervision Program	The parolee requires enhanced monitoring. At any time this condition is in effect, unless modified or withdrawn by the SISP panel, an offender shall: A. submit to electronic monitoring; B. comply with a daily activity schedule; C. not travel within or beyond county of residence without approval of supervising

		Parole Officer; D. not unlawfully use drugs, narcotics or controlled substances; E. not use intoxicating inhalants; F. not consume alcoholic beverages; G. submit to urinalysis testing; and H. obey all driving restrictions. In addition, at any time Special Condition SISP is imposed, and to the extent directed in writing by the offender's supervising Parole Officer, an offender shall: A. reside in a community residential facility (halfway house) designated by the Division and comply with all facility rules and regulations in effect during their period of residence at the facility; B. attend adult basic education program; C. attend District Reentry Center (DRC) programming; D. actively seek employment; E. not enter an establishment where the primary function is the sale and dispensing of alcoholic beverages for on-premises consumption; F. submit to alcohol use testing; G. attend substance abuse counseling sessions; H. participate in substance abuse (alcohol/narcotics) treatment program; I. attend and participate in the Special Needs Offender Program; J. take prescribed medication as directed; K. participate in anger management or counseling program; L. participate in family counseling program; M. not contact, or cause to be contacted, in person, by telephone, correspondence, video or audio device, third person, media, or by any electronic means, the victim, or guardian of the victim of instant offense; N. pay restitution as instructed; or O. inform any prospective employer of supervision status.
T	Electronic Monitoring	Offender will wear an electronic monitor.
V1	Avoiding Victim of Stalking Offense	This condition shall be imposed when the offender is serving a conviction for Texas Penal

		Code 42.072, Stalking. 1. PS I's shall review the Commitment screen to determine if the offender was convicted of the listed Texas Penal Code. 2. If the "V1" special condition is to be imposed, the PS I's shall submit a transmittal requesting a Psychological Evaluation (Special Condition P1) in accordance with Texas Government Code, Section 508.223. 3. If it is determined that the special conditions are warranted, the PS I's shall enter the appropriate special conditions (V1 and/or P1)
V2	No Contact with Victim	At any time that Special Condition "V2" is in effect, as a condition of mandatory supervision or parole, the offender not intentionally or knowingly communicate directly or indirectly with a victim of the offense, or intentionally or knowingly go near a residence, school, place of employment, or business of a victim.
X	Sex Offender Condition	At any time Special Condition "X" is in effect, the offender shall fully comply with state laws governing sex offender treatment, sex offender registration and DNA submission, internet access, child safety zone restrictions, as well as Board and Division policies governing sex offender conditions and supervision. There are many other components of Condition X and an offender does not need to have been convicted of a sex crime for the state of Texas to add Condition X to their parole.
Z	Not to Enter a Specified County	Special Condition "Z" is intended to prohibit an offender from entering a specified county without prior written approval by the parole panel.
General	Parole Fee for Certain Releasees	The offender is required to pay a parole supervision fee of $5.00 each month during the period of parole supervision.
General	Parole Supervision Fee	The offender is required to pay a parole supervision fee of $10.00 and an administrative fee of $8.00 to the Parole Division for each month the offender is under parole supervision.

Parole Approval and Denial Reasons

There are ten categories used by each board commissioner and board member to vote with a simple A for Approve or D for Deny. One or more categories may apply, but only one is required for approval or denial in the decision making process.

Rule 145.6 - Notification of Parole Panel Decision

An inmate considered for parole or mandatory supervision shall be notified of the Parole Panel's decision in writing.

Consideration and notification of the parole panel's decision includes any cumulative, pre-final consecutive sentence.

Upon considering a case for parole or mandatory supervision, the parole panel shall make a record of its decision and the reasons for its decision on the minute sheet of the inmate's file. Reasons for the parole panel's decision include but are not limited to the following:

I. Criminal History

A The record does not include a documented pattern of violent or assaultive arrests or convictions on the part of the inmate; or criminal history appears to be primarily restricted to non-violent offenses; or available information indicates only incarceration.

D The record indicates that the inmate has repeatedly committed criminal episodes or has a pattern of similar offenses that indicates a predisposition to commit criminal acts upon release; or the record indicates that the inmate is a leader or active participant in gang or organized criminal activity; or the record indicates a juvenile or adult arrest for felony or misdemeanor offenses.

II. Nature of the Offense

A The record indicates non-violent offenses; or instant offense indicates no tendency toward violent/assaultive behavior; or offense reveals limited potential for future assaultive type offenses.

D The record indicates that the inmate committed one or more violent criminal acts indicating a conscious disregard for the lives, safety, or property of others; or the instant offense or pattern of criminal activity has elements of brutality, violence, or conscious selection of victim's vulnerability such that the inmate poses a continuing threat to public safety;

III. Drug and Alcohol Involvement

A The record indicates limited or non-involvement with drug sales or usage; or the record indicates limited or non-involvement with alcohol consumption.

D The record indicates excessive drug or alcohol involvement that includes possession, use or delivery in the instant offense or criminal history.

IV. Institutional Adjustment

A The record indicates that the inmate has maintained a satisfactory institutional adjustment; i.e., no major disciplinary cases, loss of time or demotion in classification since the previous review.

D The record indicates that the inmate committed a major disciplinary offense during the preceding six months resulting in a loss of good conduct time or loss of status below that at which the inmate entered prison; or a pattern of disciplinary infractions since the last review indicates a disregard for the rules.

V. Adjustment During Periods of Supervision

A The record indicates successful periods of supervision on probation, parole, or mandatory supervision.

D The record indicates unsuccessful periods of supervision on previous probation, parole, or mandatory supervision that resulted in incarceration, including parole-inabsentia.

VI. Participation in TDCJ-CID Proposed or Specialized Programs

A The record indicates participation in and completion of TDCJ-CID proposed or specialized programs; or the inmate has completed one or more vocational or academic programs that should enhance chances to obtain and maintain full-time stable employment.

D The record indicates that the inmate refused to participate or intentionally failed to complete TDCJ-CID proposed program(s) made available to the inmate.

VII. Time Served

A The record indicates that length of time served by the inmate is congruent with offense severity and criminal history.

D The record indicates that length of time served by the inmate is not congruent with offense severity and criminal history.

VIII. Felony Offense (There is no 'A' vote)

D The record indicates that the inmate has been charged before a magistrate, indicted, or convicted by a court of competent jurisdiction, with a felony offense committed while incarcerated.

IX. Discretionary Mandatory Supervision - For a vote NOT to release, it is necessary to vote both D1 and D2, along with any other reasons that may apply.

A Release to Discretionary Mandatory Supervision

D D1 – The record indicates that the inmate's accrued good conduct time is not an accurate reflection of the inmate's potential for rehabilitation.

D2 – The record indicates that the inmate's release would endanger the public.

X. Gang Affiliation

A The record indicates that the offender is not a confirmed member of one of the TDCJ-CID designated security threat groups.

D The record indicates that the offender is a confirmed member of one of the TDCJ-CID designated security threat group.

XI. Other

A or D - Write an explanation

CHAPTER 5

PAROLE APPEAL

Appealing a parole denial is difficult, but not impossible. As long as the Parole Board can prove that it considered the statutory guidelines and relative laws in denying your parole, the courts will likely decline your appeal and uphold the parole board's denial.

But, as I said, you can and should still file an appeal of a denial of your parole, if for nothing else, to ensure that the correct information, record, and documents were used in the denial.

To do so you must first follow the internal appeal procedures by voicing your appeal to the Parole Board. In that administrative appeal, the denial will be reviewed and, possibly, reversed if you have a viable argument and have done your homework.

You only have *30 days* from the date of the parole denial to file your administrative appeal at the following address:

Texas Board of Pardons & Parole
8610 Shoal Creek Blvd.
Austin, Texas 78757
(512) 406-5864

In the event that you lose your administrative appeal, you have the right to file a Writ of Habeas Corpus (11.07) challenging the legality of your parole denial in the Court of Criminal Appeals of Texas.

There, the Court of Criminal Appeals must determine that the parole board's denial was "arbitrary and capricious" in order to reverse it. This is a very hard standard to meet, but again, it is not impossible.

And, before you ask, no, you do not have a right to an attorney during the habeas corpus process. You will have to go it alone, the best that you can. My book, "The Habeas Corpus Manual," which is available on Amazon.com and through Freebird Publishers, can provide you with a better chance of winning your habeas corpus and obtaining your parole.

The writ of habeas corpus looks like this: You can obtain the application/form from the prison law library.

Be certain to complete the entire packet and fill out and sign page 16 only. If the question does not pertain to you, or to parole specifically, leave it blank. But, as I said, a good rule of law is to fill out as much as you can, in order to give the court a good opportunity to review it.

Case No. _______________
(The district clerk of the county of conviction will fill in this blank.)

IN THE COURT OF CRIMINAL APPEALS OF TEXAS
APPLICATION FOR A WRIT OF HABEAS CORPUS
SEEKING RELIEF FROM FINAL FELONY CONVICTION
UNDER CODE OF CRIMINAL PROCEDURE ARTICLE 11.07

NAME: ____

DATE OF BIRTH: ______________________________________

PLACE OF CONFINEMENT: ______________________________

WARDEN: ____

TDCJ-CID NUMBER: ____________________ **SID NUMBER:** ____________________

(1) **This application concerns** (check all that apply):

☐ **a conviction** ☐ **parole**

☐ **a sentence** ☐ **mandatory supervision**

☐ **time credit** ☐ **out-of-time appeal or petition for discretionary review**

(2) **What are the court number and county of the district court in which you were convicted?**

____

(3) **What was the case number in the trial court?** (Put only one case number here, even if it includes multiple counts. You must make a separate application on a separate form for other case numbers.)

____

(4) **What was the name of the trial judge?**

____

(5) Were you represented by counsel? If yes, provide the attorney's name:

____

(6) What was the date that the judgment was entered?

____

(7) For what offense were you convicted and what was the sentence?

____

(8) If you were sentenced on more than one count of an indictment in the same court at the same time, what counts were you convicted of and what was the sentence in each count?

____

____

(9) What was the plea you entered? (Check one.)

- ☐ **guilty-open plea**
- ☐ **not guilty**
- ☐ **guilty-plea bargain**
- ☐ ***nolo contendere*/no contest**

If you entered different pleas to counts in a multi-count indictment, please explain:

____

____

(10) What kind of trial did you have?

- ☐ **no jury**
- ☐ **jury for guilt and punishment**
- ☐ **jury for guilt, judge for punishment**

(11) Did you testify at trial? If yes, at what phase of the trial did you testify?

____

(12) Has your sentence discharged? ☐ yes ☐ no

If you answered yes, when did your sentence discharge? ____________

(13) Did you appeal from the judgment of conviction?

☐ yes ☐ no

If you did appeal, answer the following questions:

(A) Which court of appeals decided the appeal? ____________

(B) What was the case number? ____________

(C) Were you represented by counsel on appeal? If yes, provide the attorney's name: ____________

(D) What was the decision and the date of the decision? ____________

____

(14) Did you file a petition for discretionary review in the Court of Criminal Appeals?

☐ yes ☐ no

If you did file a petition for discretionary review, answer the following questions:

(A) What was the case number? ____________

(B) What was the decision and the date of the decision? ____________

____

(15) Have you previously filed an application for a writ of habeas corpus under Article 11.07 of the Texas Code of Criminal Procedure challenging *the conviction in this case number*?

☐ yes ☐ no

If you answered yes, answer the following questions:

(A) What was the Court of Criminal Appeals' writ number? ____________
(B) What was the decision and the date of the decision? ____________

____

(C) Please briefly explain why the current grounds were not presented and could not have been presented in your previous application.

____

____

____

____

____

(16) Do you currently have any petition or appeal pending in any other state or federal court?

☐ **yes** ☐ **no**

If you answered yes, please provide the name of the court and the case number:

____

(17) If you are presenting a time credit claim, other than for pre-sentence jail time credit, have you exhausted your administrative remedies by presenting the time credit claim to the time credit resolution system of the Texas Department of Criminal Justice? (This requirement applies to any final felony conviction, including state jail felonies.)

☐ **yes** ☐ **no**

If you answered yes, answer the following questions:

(A) What date did you present the claim to the time credit resolution system?

____

(B) Did you receive a decision and, if yes, what was the date of the decision? ______

____

If you answered no, please explain why you have not presented your time credit claim to the time credit resolution system of the Texas Department of Criminal Justice:

(18) **Beginning on page 6, state concisely every legal ground for why you think that you are being illegally confined or restrained and then briefly summarize the facts supporting each ground. You must present each ground and a brief summary of the facts on the application form. If your grounds and a brief summary of the facts have not been presented on the application form, the Court will not consider your grounds. A factual summary that merely references an attached memorandum or another ground for relief will not constitute a sufficient summary of the facts.**

If you have more than four grounds, use pages 14 and 15 of the application form, which you may copy as many times as needed to give you a separate page for each ground, with each ground numbered in sequence. The recitation of the facts supporting each ground must be no longer than the two pages provided for the ground in the form.

You may include with the application form a memorandum of law if you want to present legal authorities or provide greater factual detail, but the Court will *not* consider grounds for relief set out in a memorandum of law that were not raised on the application form. The memorandum of law must comply with Texas Rule of Appellate Procedure 73 and must not exceed 15,000 words if computer-generated or 50 pages if not. If you are challenging the validity of your conviction, please include a summary of the facts pertaining to your offense and trial in your memorandum of law.

If the application form does not include all of the grounds for relief, additional grounds brought at a later date may be procedurally barred.

GROUND ONE:

____

____

FACTS SUPPORTING GROUND ONE:

____

____

____

____

____

____

____

____

____

____

____

____

____

____

GROUND TWO:

____

____

FACTS SUPPORTING GROUND TWO:

____

____

____

____

____

____

____

____

____

____

____

____

____

____

GROUND THREE:

____

____

FACTS SUPPORTING GROUND THREE:

____

____

____

____

____

____

____

____

____

____

____

____

____

____

GROUND FOUR:

____

____

FACTS SUPPORTING GROUND FOUR:

____

____

____

____

____

____

____

____

____

____

____

____

____

____

GROUND _________:

____

____

FACTS SUPPORTING GROUND:

____

____

____

____

____

____

____

____

____

____

____

____

____

____

WHEREFORE, I PRAY THAT THE COURT GRANT THE RELIEF TO WHICH APPLICANT MAY BE ENTITLED IN THIS PROCEEDING.

VERIFICATION

This application form *must be verified* in one of the following ways by either an applicant or a petitioner or it may be dismissed for noncompliance.

Applicants

In order to verify this application form, an applicant must sign one of the following:

(1) the "Unsworn Declaration" for inmates (page 16) if applicant is an inmate; or
(2) the "Unsworn Declaration" for non-inmates (page 17) if applicant is not an inmate; or
(3) the "Oath Before a Notary Public" before a notary public (page 18).

Petitioners

If a petitioner, including an attorney, presents an application form on behalf of an applicant, the petitioner may verify the application form for the applicant. In order to verify this application form, a petitioner must sign one of the following:

(1) the "Unsworn Declaration" for inmates (page 16) if petitioner is an inmate; or
(2) the "Unsworn Declaration" for non-inmates (page 17) if petitioner is not an inmate; or
(3) the "Oath Before a Notary Public" before a notary public (page 18).

In addition, *all petitioners*, including attorneys, presenting an application on behalf of an applicant must complete "Petitioner's Information" and sign "Petitioner's Statement" (page 19).

UNSWORN DECLARATION (INMATE)

My name is (First)________________ (Middle)________________(Last)________________, my date

of birth is ________________, and my inmate identifying number, if any, is ________________.

I am presently incarcerated in (Corrections unit name)________________________________ in

(City) ______________________, (County)__________________, (State) ______________,

(Zip Code)__________. I declare under penalty of perjury that the contents of this application for a

writ of habeas corpus and the facts stated in the application form are true and correct.

Executed on the ____________ day of (Month)________________ (Year)__________.

Signature of Declarant: ________________________________

UNSWORN DECLARATION (NON-INMATE)

My name is (First) _________________ (Middle) _______________ (Last)_________________, my date of birth is _______________, and my address is (Street)_________________________________ _____________________________________, (City)________________ , (State)__________, (Zip Code)__________, and (Country)_______________________. I declare under penalty of perjury that the contents of this application for a writ of habeas corpus and the facts stated in the application form are true and correct.

Executed in _________________________County, State of _______________, on the __________________day of (Month)_____________________ (Year)_____.

Signature of Declarant: ________________________________

OATH BEFORE A NOTARY PUBLIC

STATE OF TEXAS

COUNTY OF ______________

______________________________, being duly sworn, under oath says: "I am the applicant or petitioner in this action and know the contents of this application for a writ of habeas corpus and, according to my belief, the facts stated in the application form are true."

____
Signature of Declarant

SUBSCRIBED AND SWORN TO BEFORE ME THIS _____ DAY OF _________, 20_____.

____
Signature of Notary Public

PETITIONER'S INFORMATION

(Contact information for a petitioner presenting this application on behalf of the applicant)

Petitioner's printed name: ______________________________

State bar number, if applicable: ___________________________

Address: ____

____

____

Telephone: ______________________________________

Fax: ____

Email Address: ___________________________________

PETITIONER'S STATEMENT

"I am signing and presenting this application form on behalf of the applicant for the purpose of obtaining relief from the applicant's felony conviction. I have consulted with the applicant concerning this application and the applicant has given consent to the filing of this application form."

____
Signature of Petitioner

Signed on __________________, 20____.

Notes

GLOSSARY OF TERMS

Administrative Violation

A violation of one or more of the rules of parole or mandatory supervision, not including the commission of a new criminal offense. This is also known as a technical violation.

Board

Refers to the Texas Board of Pardons and Paroles.

Clemency

The power of the governor to grant a full or conditional pardon, reprieve of execution of a death sentence, commutation of a sentence, commutation of a death sentence, emergency reprieve for medical reasons, reprieve to attend civil court proceedings, or a reprieve of a jail sentence. Clemency must be recommended in writing by a majority of the Board and approved by the Governor.

Commutation of Sentence

A reduction of the penalty assessed by the court. Under Board Rules, a commutation of sentence must be supported by a majority of the applicant's trial officials, recommended in writing by a majority vote of the Board, and granted by the Governor.

Conditional Pardon

A pardon that releases the offender from confinement, subject to certain conditions. A conditional pardon may be used to request the release of an offender to another country or to immigration officials for deportation. A conditional pardon does not restore civil rights or the rights of citizenship and can be revoked by the Board if any conditions imposed were violated.

Correctional Institutions Division (CID)

The Correctional Institutions Division (CID) of the Texas Department of Criminal Justice is responsible for the confinement of adult felony offenders who are sentenced to prison.

CU/FI

Designates the date on which an offender serving consecutive or cumulative sentences will satisfy the current sentence and begin to serve the next sentence in the series. The cause number on the approved sentence will be indicated in the vote.

Deny Mandatory Supervision

A parole panel decision to deny mandatory supervision release when the panel concludes that the accrued good time is not an accurate reflection of the offender's potential for rehabilitation and that release would endanger the public. It applies to those offenders with mandatory release-eligible offenses committed on or after September 1, 1996.

Discretionary Mandatory Supervision (DMS)

A form of release that applies to certain offenders who are incarcerated for an offense committed on or after September 1, 1996, and are eligible for release on mandatory supervision. Those offenders must be approved by a parole panel for mandatory supervision release. See also HB 1433.

Emergency Reprieve

A form of executive clemency allows an offender to be temporarily released from prison for a specific reason, including, but not limited to, the offender's or a family member's medical condition. A reprieve must be recommended by a majority of the Board and approved by the Governor.

Fiscal Year (FY)

The Board's fiscal year runs from September 1 of one year through August 31 of the following year.

Full Pardon

Restoration of certain citizenship rights forfeited by law upon a criminal conviction. Citizenship rights can include the right to vote, the right to serve on a jury, and the right to hold public office.

In Texas and many states, voting rights are automatically restored when an offender discharges a felony sentence, even without a pardon, provided the offender is eligible to register. A full pardon will remove barriers to some but not all types of employment and professional licensing, but licenses are granted at the discretion of each profession's state licensing board. A pardon will not restore eligibility to become a licensed peace officer in Texas. A full pardon does not expunge a criminal record.

Further Investigation (FI)

An initial determination by a parole panel favorable to the parole release of an offender, pending further investigation. Favorable voting options are: FI-1, FI-2, FI-3R, FI-4R, FI-5, FI-6, FI- 6R, FI-7R, FI-9R, FI-18R, and CU/FI.

House Bill 1433 (HB 1433)

The law passed during the 74th Legislature requires parole panels to review scheduled mandatory supervision releases if offenses were committed on or after September 1, 1996. Specifically, HB 1433 authorizes a parole panel to review and deny mandatory supervision releases on a case-by-case basis when it determines that an offender's good conduct time does not accurately reflect the potential for rehabilitation and that the offender's release would endanger the public. See also Discretionary Mandatory Supervision.

In-Prison Therapeutic Community (IPTC)

An intensive substance abuse treatment program housed in various TDCJ CID units. As a condition of release from an IPTC, an offender is required to participate in an Aftercare Program at a Transitional Treatment Center (TTC).

Intermediate Sanction Facility (ISF)

A secure facility under contract with or operated by TDCJ that serves as a confinement alternative for offenders under active supervision who have violated one or more release conditions but have no pending charges. An ISF provides an effective addition to the range of sanctions available for parole supervision.

Mandatory Supervision (MS)

The release by law of an eligible offender when calendar time served plus good conduct time credit equals the length of the sentence. The amount of good conduct time credits determines the length of time the offender serves under the supervision of the TDCJ Parole Division.

Medically Recommended Intensive Supervision (MRIS) program

Under this program, offenders who are mentally ill, mentally retarded, elderly, terminally ill, physically handicapped, or require long-term care are considered for release by a parole panel.

Based on the offender's condition and medical evaluation, the panel may release an offender who does not constitute a threat to public safety or a threat to commit an offense.

Next Review (NR) Date

Deny parole and set a new date for the next review.

Offender

A person incarcerated in the prison system, other penal institution or jail, or a person released to parole or mandatory supervision.

Pardon

A form of executive clemency that absolves an individual from the legal consequences of their crime and conviction. A pardon must be recommended in writing by the majority of the Board and granted by the Governor.

Pardon for Innocence

The governor grants a pardon based on innocence upon the written recommendation of a majority of the Board.

Parole

The discretionary and conditional release of an eligible offender to serve the remainder of the sentence under the supervision of the TDCJ Parole Division.

Parole in Absentia (PIA)

The release of an eligible for parole or mandatory supervision offender serving a Texas sentence in an institution other than a Texas state prison, i.e., an out-of-state prison, federal facility, or municipal or county jail.

Parole Panel

A three-member panel consisting of at least one Board Member and any combination of Board Members and Parole Commissioners.

Release to Mandatory Supervision (RMS)

A decision by a parole panel to release an offender to mandatory supervision under the provisions of HB 1433 (discretionary mandatory supervision law).

Reprieve

A delay or temporary suspension of punishment. Offenders who are terminally ill or require medical treatment unavailable within TDCJ but ineligible for MRIS may seek an emergency medical reprieve. Offenders also may seek a family medical reprieve to attend to critically ill relatives. As with other forms of clemency, a reprieve requires a written recommendation from a majority of the Board and approval from the Governor. When the time allowed for a reprieve has elapsed, the offender must return to prison unless an additional reprieve is granted. Emergency reprieve requests to attend funerals or visit critically ill relatives are not handled through the executive clemency process since prison officials have the authority to grant eligible offenders short-term furloughs for such situations. In death penalty cases, the Governor may grant a reprieve for any period of time (in 30-day increments) upon recommendation of a majority of the Board. Under the Texas Constitution, the Governor has the power to grant a one-time, 30-day reprieve without the recommendation of the Board.

Restoration of Civil Rights

A form of pardon that restores all civil rights under Texas law that an offender forfeits when convicted of a federal offense, except as specifically provided in the certificate of restoration (Texas Code of Criminal Procedure Section 48.05 - Restoration of Civil Rights). An offender may apply for restoration of civil rights after completing their sentence if they were convicted three or more years before the date of application and if they have no other conviction under the laws of Texas, another state, or the United States.

Revocation

A parole panel decides to return an offender to the custody of the TDCJ CID because the offender has violated the terms or conditions of release, committed a new crime, or both.

Serve-All (SA)

Deny parole with no subsequent review, requiring the offender to serve the balance of sentence, unless eligible for mandatory supervision consideration.

Sex Offender

Offenders who have been convicted of or transferred from juvenile parole or commitment to adult parole or prison for an offense in Chapter 21, Penal Code; required to register pursuant to Chapter 62, Code of Criminal Procedure; or constituted a threat to society by reason of lack of sexual control. This definition does not apply to defendants currently on or discharged a deferred adjudication community supervision.

Substance Abuse Felony Punishment Facility (SAFPF)

A secure chemical-dependence treatment facility under contract with the TDCJ for non-violent offenders. An offender may be placed in a SAFPF by a parole panel as a condition of parole or mandatory supervision following a hearing.

Super Intensive Supervision Program (SISP)

The highest level of supervision and offender accountability under the TDCJ Parole Division, created by the 75th Legislature for potentially dangerous offenders released on parole or mandatory supervision.

Technical Violation

A violation of one or more of the rules of parole or mandatory supervision, not including a new criminal offense. This is also known as an administrative violation.

Texas Department of Criminal Justice (TDCJ)

An umbrella agency that includes the Community Justice Assistance Division, the Correctional Institutions Division, and the Parole Division.

A MOMENT WITH THE AUTHOR

In a recent interview that I provided to the News Agency, I was asked: Why do you write books that help inmates when you have been successful with other verticals?

My answer was simple: Because inmates need help, prison reform can only be achieved from the inside out.

The biggest misconception inmates have is that those on the outside know what happens on the inside. Trust me, they do not, and in most cases, they believe only what they are told by prison officials and the administration.

For instance, look at the Texas Department of Criminal Justice (TDJC) online food menu, which is available to the public. There, you will see food such as Chicken Fried Steak, Smothered Beef Roll, Chicken Bake Casserole, etc., none of which we ever really receive.

Yet, the public believes that we actually eat like that.

So, how do we educate the public and bring forth change? It begins by educating *yourself.*

Prison is seen in two different lights—one, as a punishment, and two, as an opportunity. Your attitude determines which, and thus how you will live your prison life: Hard or Easy.

Nearly all state correctional departments have and provide educational programs and certifications. I know for a fact that the Federal prison system does. And now, the Federal Government has re-instituted the Inmate Pell Grant which will provide educational funding at no expense to you.

Gone are your excuses for being lazy and underachieving. Gone are your reasons and justifications for complaining.

Over the course of my nearly nine years in prison, and for a crime I did not commit and fight to reverse every minute of my life here, I have used education to mount that fight. I cannot expect to be heard unless I speak the language that my captors speak. That the appellate courts speak: Legalese.

That is learned in school, as well as in my publications.

Changing your situation begins with changing *yourself.* Changing your way of thinking, the way that you see your incarceration, the way that you respond to your incarceration.

Like life, prison is 1% what happened to us and 99% how we respond to what has happened to us. If those numbers are in reverse for you, you are not on the right path and are unlikely to obtain relief or parole.

Take, for instance, the purpose of this book: *Parole.*

In the beginning, and because it is legally required, I told you to seek an Attorney to assist you in preparing your parole packet if you are financially able to do so.

Later, I shared with you the response of Mr. Long, a top administration official for parole here in Texas. He said flat-out that he and the other members of the parole board look more favorable on the parole packet prepared by an inmate *without an attorney.*

I followed that by supporting his position because I can understand the reasoning and purpose of his statement: Officials and the Administration want to see your incentive and commitment.

They want to see that you care and are willing to try. They do not judge your parole packet, nor do they refuse it. Hell, they do not even require it; they prefer it.

It's about initiative and attempt. Standing on your own. It's about whether you care enough even to try.

That is why I have written this book: to teach you how to fight for yourself. I truly believe that you can and will.

In more than 50+ years of my life, I have learned one most important lesson: When we know better, we usually do better.

It is my responsibility and privilege, as well as that of Freebird Publishers, to stand with you and teach you. Take, for instance, the Article at the end of this letter to you. It describes the fight and stance that Freebird and I take against prison policies and laws all across the United States.

Together, we have been instrumental and highly successful in reaching all of you, teaching all of you, and using our combined voices and knowledge to change the system and get you the relief you need, want, and deserve.

That is why I write the books, write and file the House Bills across the United States, appeal to Senators and Congressional Leaders, and file Federal Impact Litigation. *It is my duty.*

To you, as well as to myself, a human being is not really a human being until they are in voluntary service to and for another human being without any expectation, lending a helping hand, carrying the burden, or blazing the path for the less fortunate or incapable.

I do not have the privilege of Mandatory release nor does Freebird Publishers. But that does not, has not, and will not stop us from fighting the fight for you, as the following article provides. We are in service to you.

All that we ask is that you pick up the sword and fight beside us and with us for the benefit of all inmates through your dedication to learning. Action = Results.

Your purchase of this book tells me that you have the desire, motivation, initiative, and fight to obtain the relief you desire. *Good for you*!

Life is simple, even prison life.
Either you are the bug, or you are the windshield.
It's as simple as that.

Our spiritual beliefs, no matter what faith you are (they all say the same thing), tell us that faith without works/action is dead. It is not injured, not hard, not impossible. *It is dead!*

I tell you this, my brothers and sisters, *you are capable*. And I *believe in you*.

Now flip this book over and read it again. Memorize it, practice it, and then go and get what you have earned and likely deserve since you are even eligible for it: *Parole*.

Good Luck!

Also, for all of you Texas inmates, I highly recommend that you contact Attorney Robert Virden with any of your Will, Trust, and Probate matters before you sign anything that your family members want you to sign.

Not only is he a great lawyer, he is a good man and will have your best interest at heart. He will review your matters pro bono (without cost) and then provide you with further advice. I am privileged to call him my friend. Keep your letters brief, accurate, and concise.

Please do not bother him with legal matters related to criminal or appellate law; he *cannot help you*.

Mr. Robert N. Virden, P.C.
Attorney at Law
3419 Westminster Avenue
Dallas, Texas 75205-1387

214-373-7161 Office
214-537-2229 Mobile

Mandatory Releases Begin for State Prisoners

Freebird Publishers Leads the Way for Prisoners Seeking Mandatory Release

North Dighton, MA -- (ReleaseWire) -- 02/09/2023 --In the wake of the Mandatory Release of state prisoners, Alabama Attorney General Steve Marshall files suit to obstruct the prisoner's early release. Likewise, Alabama Governor Kay Ivey goes on record that she continues to stand for public safety. This political stance by elected officials is common among all the states around the country. They are strong on the pro-prison stance but continually obstruct state-sponsored rehabilitation. Thus, our elected officials continue to convict the poor rather than fight the poverty that leads to crime. Freebird Publishers (https://www.freebirdpublishers.com/product-page/2254-pro-se-guide-to-winning-federal-relief) does and continues to stand for American Prisoners in need of help. They provide information that helps prisoners find rehabilitation and early release from state and federal prisons. This is best exemplified by their distribution of books by the nationally known author Raymond E. Lumsden.

In Mr. Lumsden's line of books, prisoners will find many ways to fight for early release from prison in state and federal courts. His books consist of:

The Habeas Corpus Manual
This book is written specifically for the pro se inmate. Within its pages lay the information, process, and instructions for obtaining relief in a state habeas corpus.

From the initial investigation through filing a writ of habeas corpus, prisoners are provided effective forms, motions, and detailed instructions specific to state-level habeas corpus.

Armed with this book, relief is only a few pages away if done properly and effectively. Any pro se inmate serious about post-conviction relief should order a copy. Even if not incarcerated or are not an inmate and looking to overturn a conviction, sentence, etc., this is the book needed.

§ 2254 Pro Se Guide to Winning Federal Relief

Designed to teach and assist pro se prisoners, and the public, in post-conviction proceedings. This extremely easy-to-use tutorial is packed full of sample motions, letters, forms, and pleadings that will assist in advancing one's rights in federal court. It's a must-have for anyone attempting to do so pro se.

Logically written in layman's terms for easy comprehension and strategically outlined and organized, this book allows people to absorb and easily follow the complicated and twisted path that is the federal court system.

This is an invaluable tool and resource for any pro se user who hopes to achieve relief in their federal post-conviction habeas corpus. Herein is everything you will ever need to know, at your fingertips for use and application, in a federal habeas corpus.

Media Relations Contact

Diane E. Schindelwig
CEO
Freebird Publishers
1-774-406-8682

Email | Web | Profile

Follow Freebird Publishers

Freebird Publishers - Logo

Related Images

The Pro Se Guide to Legal Research & Writing
This easy-to-follow and understand guide provides everyone with the tools necessary to obtain relief from legal issues.

Clear, concise, and direct legal writing is essential for inmates.
Prison "writ-writers" use opaque, jargon-filled writing, which only further alienates those reading it. In this manner, relief is hard-pressed to obtain, if at all.

This book, created for inmates, is the most practical and effective manual available for pro se use.
Every inmate should own a copy and many already do.

The Pro Se Section 1983 Manual

This book is an invaluable and indispensable resource for the pro se inmate seeking to protect their constitutional rights in prison and obtain reform. Comprehensive, precise, and layman guidance provides pro se inmates with information regarding:

" Conditions of Confinement
" Civil Rights in Prison
" Due Process
" How to Litigate
" Legal Research
" Preparing Legal Documents

Written by an inmate for inmates, the Pro Se Section 1983 manual is an authoritative, organized, and easy-to-understand manual designed to bring results and relief. Every inmate wishing to protect their civil rights should have a copy. There is no other book like this one related to Section 1983.

For more information about how a prisoner can exercise their rights, visit www.freebirdpublishers.com.

About Freebird Publishers
Freebird Publishers (https:// www.freebirdpublishers.com) is headquartered in North Dighton, Massachusetts (MA). They serve the entire United States and international locations. They have earned the confidence of prisoners and their families nationwide by being a leader in the business of providing necessary information and specialized publishing services to inmates and their loved ones since 2013. Freebird Publishers provides a full listing of the hundreds of services available to prisoners in their detailed publication, the "Inmate Shopper". For more information about the "Inmate Shopper" and the tools, it provides that an inmate can use to make their incarceration productive visit: https://www.freebirdpublisher.com or send a direct email to: Diane@freebirdpublishers.com, also accessible to inmates using prisoner email systems.

ABOUT THE AUTHOR

Raymond E. Lumsden continues to fight his wrongful conviction and sentence within the Texas Department of Criminal Justice. He also continues to fight for prison reform through impact civil rights litigation(s) in the federal courts of Texas, the Fifth Circuit Court of Appeals, and the United States Supreme Court.

This is his fifth book in a *pro se* legal series dedicated to educating and assisting *pro se* litigants in their post-conviction, civil rights, criminal law, and legal research & writing pursuits. Raymond is extensively educated, trained, and certified in all areas of law. He is completing his Juris Doctor Program and recently graduated from a three-year Astrology

Program with Honors. Like a true Sagittarius, Raymond's thirst for knowledge and education is unquenchable. Soon, he will begin a two-year correspondence program in Advanced Forensic DNA Study while also pursuing a Psychology Degree.

Raymond is a Minnesota-raised Native and a diehard Chicago Bears Fan. In the past, he has appeared on the Oprah Winfrey Show, Joey Reynold's National Radio Show, Judge Mathis, Prison Break, and CSI Miami, and has appeared in numerous motion pictures such as "The Dead Don't Scream" (2007). Raymond authored a memoir in 2007 titled, "Stronger By The Day," that won two awards and was optioned for screenplay rights.

More importantly, Raymond is the proud father of Anthony, Alyssa, Joshua, and Rylee. He has two grandchildren, Rysen and Aniyah.

FREEBIRD PUBLISHERS

Thanks for your interest in Freebird Publishers!

We value our customers and would love to hear from you! Reviews are an important part in bringing you quality publications. We love hearing from our readers-rather it's good or bad (though we strive for the best)!

If you could take the time to review/rate any publication you've purchased with Freebird Publishers we would appreciate it!

If your loved one uses Amazon, have them post your review on the books you've read. This will help us tremendously, in providing future publications that are even more useful to our readers and growing our business.

Amazon works off of a 5 star rating system. When having your loved one rate us be sure to give them your chosen star number as well as a written review. Though written reviews aren't required, we truly appreciate hearing from you.

Sample Review Received on Inmate Shopper

poeticsunshine

Truly a guide

Reviewed in the United States on June 29, 2023

Verified Purchase

This book is a powerhouse of information. My son had to calm/ground himself to prioritize where to start.

Made in United States
North Haven, CT
04 November 2026

21728192R00120